MISSION IN THE MARKETPLACE

Perspectives for Life and Work

Jeffrey W. Comment

MITM Publishing

First printing August 1995

ISBN 0-9647405-0-8

Printed in
the United States of America

MITM Publishing
P. O. Box 12523
North Kansas City, MO 64116

*Thanks to my family
and all my friends for
their encouragement*

CONTENTS

Acknowledgments

Preface

1. Looking at the Perfect Management Style
How does your management style compare to
Christ's? Are you managing from strength or
weakness?

2. The Bottom Line
How do we measure up to God's priorities? Are we
overachievers, underachievers, or God's
achievers?

3. Ethics and the Balance Sheet
How do we apply God's moral and ethical standards
to business?

4. Anger in the Boardroom
How do we love those who don't love us?

5. Conducting Business With the Opposite Sex
How do we work with the opposite sex in the business
environment?

6. Taking a Recess From Stress
How does stress affect us? How would God want us to
deal with stress?

ACKNOWLEDGMENTS

To Martha, my wife for twenty-five years,
who was always there.

To Jim Hughey, who was the first person to catch the
vision and stay with it for the long haul.

To Shifra Stein and Mike Anderson, who brought the
work to completion.

To Russ Cadle and Neil Atkinson, my good friends
who encouraged me to finish what I started.

PREFACE

This book is the result of an odyssey that began almost ten years ago. That was when I learned that, after nine years of hard work, I was about to lose my job as president of John Wanamaker. One morning, while taking the train from Philadelphia to our new parent organization in Washington, D.C., I reflected on my life. I felt sorry for myself, and it was painful for me to deal with the reality that I was no longer needed, or wanted.

I asked God one of the most frequently asked questions: "Why me?"

It was almost as if I heard an audible voice answer me. "If you listen, you will understand." It was a feeling that was so absolute that I couldn't ignore it. It got my attention. I felt that over the next few months God was going to share with me some important insights on how He wanted me to live my life.

It was as if a light turned on in my head. I had never really taken time to reflect on how God worked in my life. Thoughts flooded my mind. I got out a pencil and began to write. This was the beginning of a year of uncertainty, as my job as president of John Wanamaker was being phased out. It was at this time that I began to put down my thoughts on paper. The process was truly the beginning of a life-changing experience for me.

As I looked back over the years, I could see clear evidence of God's involvement in my life. I saw how my experiences had drawn me closer to Him. It was a fascinating exercise. I became aware, through my writing, that God was encouraging me, and I, in turn, wanted to do the same for others.

Coincidentally I was introduced to Jim Hughey at a meeting in Philadelphia. Jim, who was in charge of development at the Dallas Seminary back then, was the first of several people who were to influence this work. During the course of our conversation, I told Jim about my writing, and he asked to see my work. He seemed excited by what he read and encouraged me to organize my thoughts more cohesively. Although neither one of us considered ourselves writers, we began to shape the material into what we felt might become a potential book. About a year later the first phase of Mission in the Marketplace began to take shape.

Jim and I were energized by what we were doing, yet others didn't seem to share our enthusiasm, including publishers who were polite but uninterested in the project. I began to think that perhaps this idea was inspirational for me alone, and so I put the book idea aside and began to live my life around the words I had written.

That's when my life began to change.

The material sat on the shelf for five years until I met a nationally published journalist and author named Shifra Stein. My religious experience as well as Jim's was rooted in our faith with Christ; hers was a Jewish background. Shifra impressed me with having a deep desire to find the full meaning of life. I shared some of my work with her and she said to me, "Jeff, I think what you've written is terrific and I believe it has a message for many people, regardless of their faith. I'd like to help you complete what you started."

Finally, it all came together when Shifra introduced me to a graphic designer named Mike Anderson. Mike, a committed Christian, was excited by the possibility of a book, saying that designing the book and coordinating the publication of the work was something he felt strongly compelled to do.

Somehow the four of us, Jim, Shifra, Mike, and myself, were brought together for a reason. We all felt that this work was something special, and I knew that God was telling me to complete my labor of love.

My prayer is that this book will encourage Christians, especially those in the marketplace, to be the men and women He has called us to be. I also pray that this work might help each of us develop a clear and better understanding of the sovereign plan He has for our lives.

Jeffrey W. Comment

Chapter One

LOOKING AT THE PERFECT MANAGEMENT STYLE

D o you remember your big promotion? The job you worked for and dreamed about for all those years? The day the boss walked in and said, "You got it!"

That dream came true for me when I became president of John Wanamaker's, a chain of department stores in the Philadelphia area. I moved from Florida to Pennsylvania with one goal in mind: to be president of that company. Now I had made it. I was excited! It felt good to be the president.

My first thought was, "I want to leave my mark on this company." I needed to show my boss I was special and that his decision to put me in charge was a good one. I began looking for trouble spots. It didn't take long to find a major problem.

The furniture department was a significant contributor to sales, but poor productivity and substandard customer service kept it from being profitable. The situation was threatening our reputation as a company that cared for its clientele.

To me the basic problem was that the home-delivery drivers were indifferent to our customer needs. We had to make

How does your management style compare to Christ's?

Are you managing from strength or weakness?

1

Chapter One

customers a top priority, thus enhancing service to our clients.

I made my first major presidential decision. I fired the Teamster drivers and struck a deal with an independent trucking company to deliver our furniture. I believed this change would reduce costs substantially and improve service to our customers.

Here I was, the brash, take-charge president, making what I thought was a sound business decision that made good business sense. I never dreamed what was about to happen would merit a chapter in the company's history. I was going to leave a mark on John Wanamaker's, all right. Not for improving the business, but for starting a war!

Unfortunately I never considered the impact of firing the Teamsters. Through a third-party trucking company they had been the home-delivery drivers for Wanamaker's furniture department for almost twenty years. In Philadelphia the Teamsters reign, and their leaders do not appreciate members being without jobs.

All of a sudden it seemed as if everyone in Philadelphia belonged to a union and all were madly in love with the Teamsters. I quickly found that my dismissing these drivers was tantamount to the Japanese bombing of Pearl Harbor.

For the next three months my office became a command post as we battled for the right to serve customers without harassment. Property damage ran into thousands of dollars, and several people on both sides received physical injuries.

Toward the end of the strike our trucks were making deliveries escorted by police. I was being verbally abused as well as publicly threatened, and had to install twenty-four-hour security surveillance around my home. I've never experienced that kind of hostility before or since. It was a real mess. People looked to me for answers, but to be honest, I didn't have a clue as to where to turn. I was crushed, humiliated, and felt totally foolish.

I thought I had done my homework, covering all our bases

from the beginning. We'd gotten legal advice from some of the best law firms in Philadelphia, and our own legal counsel and corporate staff were all in agreement. However, this made no difference in the outcome.

We took the problem to court. Unfortunately the political influence of the union and their elected supporters prevented any possible relief through the legal system. Our leverage with another Teamster union, the warehouse workers, was unraveling as they shifted their support to their sister union, the drivers. A work stoppage looked imminent.

Now the parent corporation was starting to question my judgment. The poor press we received did not help. I was asked more than once why I didn't do my homework and why I hadn't anticipated this kind of problem.

Emotionally I was about to explode. Finally I sat down and prayed, "God, I guess I blew this one. I need your help."

When the whole mess seemed to be at its worst and it looked like we were definitely going to have a strike by the warehouse people, I received a phone call. The caller, a man I had met briefly the year before and who really knew me only by name, was a labor arbitrator. But more importantly, he knew the attorneys for the Teamsters. He offered to try and bring both parties together if I was willing. Was I ever willing!

In less than forty-eight hours this man, who I later discovered was a committed Christian, brought the Teamsters and us together. After an all-night session, we reached a compromise agreement. The Teamsters were back on our trucks, but at new rates with a new third-party trucking company and a commitment to customer service. Finally, after ninety days and over $2 million in losses, the strike was over and neither side felt it had lost.

Since that day I've often wondered how Christ would have dealt with the Teamsters. How would He have handled a labor situation that got out of hand?

Although I was very thankful the negotiations resulted in a settlement, it wasn't until almost a year later that my new friend,

Chapter One

the labor arbitrator, asked me if I had ever talked to the Teamsters' local president after the strike.

"You've got to be kidding!" I said. "I wouldn't want to be in the same room with that guy!"

All I could remember were some pretty unpleasant things he said about me and the anguish he had caused our company, customers, and associates.

My friend's response shattered my righteous indignation.

"You need to talk to that man for several reasons," he said. "First, I think the Bible says something about harboring anger and not forgiving. Second, neither one of you was 100 percent right on the deal. And finally, you'll have to negotiate another contract in two years."

I knew he was correct on all three counts. After several days of procrastination I called the local president of the Teamsters and invited him to lunch. I think he was as surprised to receive my call as I was making it.

Our lunch turned out to be a three-hour affair with more great Italian dishes than I knew existed. We had an enjoyable time, and I discovered one very important lesson: Never try to judge a person's behavior until you understand the principles that determine his every act. Discovering another person's perspective enabled me to learn some incredible things about the local Teamsters and their leader.

While I didn't agree with all their principles or their actions, at least I understood why they did some of the things they did during the strike. In return, I had a chance to give my own viewpoint. Would you believe we even shared our faiths and talked about our families?

At the end of our lunch, we agreed never to take any action involving the other without first sitting down and talking face to face. I'm convinced that if I had a problem with that union today, I could call the local Teamster president and it could be resolved. I feel confident today that if confronted with labor contract negotiations, I would conduct myself much differently.

Our job is not necessarily to agree with the opposition, but we do have the responsibility to understand their position. Only then can we weigh all the facts and act accordingly. That's what our associates expect, our shareholders deserve, and God demands.

MANAGING IN A CHRIST-LIKE WAY

Managing in a Christ-like way should have been my goal in making the delivery driver decision. Obviously, it was not. Looking back, I have to admit I made a lot of mistakes in reaching that decision. Ego became a factor, and clearly I was not as sensitive as I should have been to people. I learned from this experience by objectively asking myself, "What did I do right? What did I do wrong?"

I think we need to also ask ourselves how Jesus would make decisions in today's free enterprise system. What would His management style look like?

I've always believed that one of the greatest and most essential attributes of a leader is the ability to manage and motivate people to significantly improve the organization and environment in which they operate.

There are many books and theories on how to lead and manage people, and we can learn some excellent human resource techniques from them. But one of the greatest books on human resource management—and one many Christians forget—is the Bible, especially in the life and teachings of Jesus Christ.

So how would Jesus lead today? We need to know so we can be better leaders in our organizations. We need to know so we may lead in His image.

The most visible demonstration of Jesus' leadership strength was in His relationship with the Apostles. Twelve men brought together by Jesus Christ—seemingly ordinary by all standards—changed the world. They included an unknown fisherman, a despised tax collector, and a thief who would betray the Master.

How would Jesus make decisions in today's free enterprise system? What would His management style look like?

Chapter One

Jesus recruited, trained, and led this ragtag band through three years of ministry, then left behind the most significant management team ever put together in the history of the world! A management team that would have to finish their task without the personal presence of their leader! Jesus Christ Inc., as I like to refer to the Apostles, would be a viable company for more than 2,000 years.

I like to study the life of Christ in the Gospel of Luke. The only Gentile author of Scripture, Luke was a medical doctor and wrote an orderly account of the life of our Savior. Although not an eyewitness to any of the events described in his account, he carefully investigated his work to prove the certainty of the gospel message. But I mainly like Luke because he brings out the human side of Jesus. His leadership characteristics jump out as you see Him in a more vivid way. In Luke, Jesus embodies seven significant management traits. As you read through them here, ask yourself these questions:

• If I understood and lived the leadership characteristics of Jesus, would I be a better leader in my organization?

• Would I be more like Jesus?

SEVEN SIGNIFICANT MANAGEMENT TRAITS AS EXEMPLIFIED BY JESUS

1. Mission With a Passion

Jesus understood His own mission and purpose on earth. In Luke 4, Jesus publicly described His ministry for the first time while teaching in Nazareth. Today we would say He gave His mission statement:

The Spirit of the Lord is on me, because he has anointed me to preach good news to the poor. He has sent me to proclaim freedom for the prisoners and recovery of sight for the blind, to release the oppressed, to proclaim the year of the Lord's favor. Luke 4:18-19

Later in chapter 4, after healing Peter's mother-in-law and many others in Capernaum, Jesus sought solitude but was beseeched by the people to stay in their midst. He again stated

the reason for His being on earth. You can feel His passion as
He says,

*I must preach the good news of the kingdom of God to the
other towns also, because that is why I was sent.* Luke 4:43

Jesus knew why He was there. He did not keep His mission
to Himself; He built it into the lives of His followers. Jesus gave
His disciples clear direction with an understandable purpose—
they knew where their leader was going. Although they often
became confused and at times unbelieving, Jesus did not allow
His disciples to wander too far. He never led them without
telling them where He was going and eventually where they
must go as well.

In Luke 10, Jesus carefully explains the mission and purpose
He would have for His disciples, then gave them a practical lesson:

*After this the Lord appointed seventy-two others and sent
them two by two ahead of him to every town and place where he
was about to go. He told them, "The harvest is plentiful, but the
workers are few. Ask the Lord of the harvest, therefore, to send
out workers into his harvest field. Go! I am sending you out like
lambs among wolves. Do not take a purse or bag or sandals;
and do not greet anyone on the road.*

*"When you enter a house, first say, 'Peace to this house.' If a
man of peace is there, your peace will rest on him; if not, it will
return to you. Stay in that house, eating and drinking whatever
they give you, for the worker deserves his wages. Do not move
around from house to house.*

*"When you enter a town and are welcomed, eat what is set
before you. Heal the sick who are there and tell them, 'The kingdom of God is near you.' But when you enter a town and are not
welcomed, go into its streets and say, 'Even the dust of your
town that sticks to our feet we wipe off against you. Yet be sure
of this: The kingdom of God is near.' I tell you, it will be more
bearable on that day for Sodom than for that town.*
Luke 10:1-12

Chapter One

Then He added:

"He who listens to you listens to me; he who rejects you rejects me; but he who rejects me rejects him who sent me." Luke 10:16

What a great example of a leader with a mission and a leader who instills that mission in His followers. The results are reported in the next verse of chapter 10:

The seventy-two returned with joy and said, "Lord, even the demons submit to us in your name." Luke 10:17

The seventy-two understood their mission and performed accordingly. Jesus not only told them where they were going, He told them why. He gave them purpose. The results are history.

When I take a look at businesses and organizations across America today, one thing is missing in many of them: They don't understand their mission. Without that basic understanding, it is impossible to have much direction or passion. Does your company or organization have a mission statement? Do you know what your mission is?

I remember when I joined the John Wanamaker Company in Philadelphia. I had read about the founder, John Wanamaker, and the mission he had for his store in the late 1800s. He envisioned one-stop shopping, with all retail categories under one roof. His ultimate dream was single-price retailing. Believe it or not, the ideas he implemented over a century ago were still guiding our company 100 years later. With some changes to John's original plan of action and some great new internal marketing, we were in a position to enable 7,000 associates to understand the John Wanamaker Company's goals of today.

On the other hand, when I arrived at Helzberg Diamonds, I realized our business had no cohesive plan of action and had not defined its goals. It hadn't taken a real inventory of its assets and didn't know where it was headed. As I look back on these two very different companies, I can see that major differences existed.

John Wanamaker had a clearly defined mission; however, it hadn't challenged sufficiently the viability of its objectives. The John Wanamaker concept in the early 1900s was innovative and leading edge. In 1980, it was obsolete and uncompetitive. As a consequence, the store achieved only mediocre results.

As for Helzberg Diamonds, it initially did not have a clear mission statement. After much review, however, the company began to understand who it was, what its niche should be, and what it wanted to accomplish. The result was that Helzberg Diamonds became, in the long run, much more successful than John Wanamaker in achieving its goals.

Why? Because Helzberg Diamonds' mission in the jewelry industry made sense and the company's goals were logical. It's not enough just to have a mission statement; your mission statement must fit who you are and take into consideration the correct business environment and today's needs.

At Helzberg Diamonds we have a one-sentence mission statement, which every management person, from the CEO to each store manager, understands. The statement is very simple and to the point. Every manager is expected to understand our objectives and be able to determine if each task he or she performs is fulfilling our plan of action.

We should all be asking ourselves those same kinds of questions. I also believe that, without a mission statement to give direction and purpose for our lives, we cannot have the passion to bring success to our organization.

The Helzberg Diamonds mission statement first states who we are and what we want to accomplish. This is what I call the meat and potatoes of the mission statement. We then add the basic principles of how we intend to accomplish our mission. These are important in keeping us on track. Each statement is clear, concise, and to the point. Most importantly, it's simple to understand. With that in mind, I'd like to share the Helzberg Diamonds mission statement with you.

Compare our mission statement to your company's (Appendix, pages 142 & 143). Does it raise your level of pas sion?

> It's not enough just to have a mission statement; your mission statement must fit who you are .

Chapter One

Jesus knew His mission and He had a passion for it. His disciples could see it; they could feel it as He sent them into the world. He clearly stated his objective and backed it up with authority. Imagine Him standing in front of the seventy-two, sending them into a world that could and probably would be hostile. He wasn't sending them out with suggestions on what to do. He gave them a charge, a command to do the job. No options—just do it!

If you don't understand your mission, you can't have a passion for your job. That's what is missing from many companies in our free enterprise system today. Think of Christ's mission: it had enough power behind it to last for eternity. Jesus was a leader who gave firm and concise direction. A leader also gives his associates a purpose and a passion to accomplish their goals.

The great business leaders of today have those leadership characteristics. They give their companies direction and a sense of purpose. More importantly, they model those characteristics for their associates.

Associates that get that kind of leadership inevitably will have some of the disciples' characteristics. If our associates today felt that same sense of ownership and involvement as the disciples did, I believe the loyalty that is missing now in many corporations would return.

The same can be said of the Christian community. Many Christian organizations do not know their mission as stated in the Bible. Many have lost their passion for the Author of their mission. When we have no passion for Christ, it shows. That same lack of passion spills over into other parts of our lives and we lose our zeal for the things that go with living a life of character and integrity that sets us apart from the world.

Remember we are here to glorify Christ in all we do and in the process be changed to reflect Him more and more each day.

2. Focus and Understanding

Jesus was focused and made sure His apostles understood

what He was about. His strategy was specific and clearly understandable to those who met Him, regardless of whether they would follow Him or not. The Apostles knew exactly what was expected of them as they walked beside Him.

A great illustration of this appears in Luke 5, where Jesus explains who He is and what His people exemplify. Jesus made it clear that He did not come to patch the old system of the law, but to bring an entire new system of relating to God:

They said to him, "John's disciples often fast and pray, and so do the disciples of the Pharisees, but yours go on eating and drinking."

Jesus answered,

Can you make the guests of the bridegroom fast while he is with them? But the time will come when the bridegroom will be taken from them; in those days they will fast.

Then He gave them this illustration:

And no one pours new wine into old wineskins. If he does, the new wine will burst the skins, the wine will run out and the wineskins will be ruined. No, new wine must be poured into new wineskins. And no one after drinking old wine wants the new, for he says, "The old is better." Luke 5:33-35, 37-39

Again in Luke 9, Jesus gives the Apostles practical application similar to the direction He gave to the seventy-two disciples. He draws their attention to the mission statement and sends them out to minister on His behalf:

When Jesus had called the Twelve together, he gave them power and authority to drive out all demons and to cure diseases, and he sent them out to preach the kingdom of God and to heal the sick. He told them: "Take nothing for the journey— no staff, no bag, no bread, no money, no extra tunic. Whatever house you enter, stay there until you leave that town. If people do not welcome you, shake the dust off your feet when you leave their town, as a testimony against them." So they set out and went from village to village, preaching the gospel and healing people everywhere. Luke 9:1-6

Chapter One

The direction that He gave to the inner circle of twelve was the same as He gave to the multitude. He was focused. In my job I strive to give the same direction to our executive committee that I do to our associates. It is a shame that today so many businesses are not clear with regard to their goals. General, broad-brush strategies are dangerous and can almost paralyze an organization and its people. When you don't understand what you are supposed to do, you run the great risk of doing the wrong thing or nothing at all. People will be less likely to take risks when they are unsure of themselves or the focus of their company.

Jesus made the disciples feel like they were part of His mission and let them know they were important in accomplishing it.

Our own free enterprise system has some classic examples of both large and small companies that started with a specific focus but over time began to lose their vision. The automobile industry in America is probably our most visible example. I think people in that business would agree that one of the major reasons why the European and Japanese automakers have made such inroads in market share over the last decade was our lack of focus on what the consumer really wanted. Fortunately for the American automobile industry, this fact was recently recognized and the clarity that was lost is being restored.

There have also been problems regarding retail stores. Sears, Roebuck and Company is a classic example of a company with a tremendous market share that began to diversify into other industries, many times into businesses with no connection to retailing. The result was a loss of focus on its customers and a fragmented approach to its market. Sears's confusion opened the door for a little upstart competitor to begin chipping away at its customer base. Now that competitor, WalMart, is the largest retailer in America.

In my business people always ask me why we don't carry china or silver. I have a very simple answer. We're a jewelry specialty business, and this is our only focus. All our associates understand that philosophy. This simply frees them up to become experts in one specific area. We believe in the proven theory that organizations with clear goals perform better.

Making sure our associates understand our focus is important to us. After Jesus' death and resurrection, the confidence demonstrated by the disciples shows us the significance of Christ choosing a clear ministry direction. The Book of Acts, written as a sequel to the Gospel of Luke, reveals Jesus' success with the disciples. Jesus made the disciples feel like they were a part of His mission and let them know they were important in accomplishing that mission. Because they had ownership in the mission, His disciples were incredibly loyal, even after He was gone.

I think Jesus would have loved the "wheelbarrow story," a scientific study conducted in the 1950s. It emphasizes the need for our associates to understand our goals and how they can contribute. Let me share it with you:

On each of two assembly lines, one person fills a wheelbarrow with parts and takes it to the other end of the assembly line, empties it, and returns for another load. One of the workers is told why the task is being performed, the other is not. The outcome is that the worker who knows why he is doing the work is 50 percent more productive.

Every time we write a memo in our company giving our associates a task, we always include a "wheelbarrow" clause. This tells recipients why we are asking them to do the job and that we consider their participation important. In this way our associates are made to feel they are providing a valuable service—which they are!

In the Appendix, page 144, is a copy of a company memo carrying a "wheelbarrow" paragraph. Using the wheelbarrow concept, you can give your associates real support. Jesus also supported his followers, making them feel needed and necessary. Can you imagine how much more productive we could be if we had the focus and understanding He modeled? Can you imagine how your business or organization would look?

3. Teacher and Trainer

Jesus was a great teacher and trainer who must have looked at the wide diversity of His apostles as an asset. He had a whole new way of life to teach them and He could almost start from ground zero.

Chapter One

Although His ministry was to the people, the Bible often reflects on the many times He pulled His apostles aside and spent quality time in teaching, training, and equipping them so they might become the men He desired them to be.

After he sent the twelve out and they returned, Jesus' first reaction was to take them aside. He listened to what they had accomplished. The disciples were with Him constantly as He prayed and ministered.

Of course the most well-known teaching trait of Jesus was His use of parables. When His apostles asked why He used parables, His response was straightforward, as found in Luke 8:

The knowledge of the secrets of the kingdom of God has been given to you, but to others I speak in parables, so that, "though seeing, they may not see; though hearing, they may not understand." Luke 8:10

Even today nothing explains a position on an idea better than a short story, or as I call it, a "word picture." I've seen this concept incorporated in training programs with great success. As one of our salespeople once told me, our training programs that use word pictures are relevant. They aren't just philosophy; they are practical concepts that enhance our ability to close the sale.

Again in Luke 9:28-36, we see another method of Jesus' teaching and training the Apostles, which was simply spending quality time with His people:

About eight days after Jesus said this, he took Peter, John, and James and went up onto a mountain to pray. As he was praying, the appearance of his face changed, and his clothes become as bright as a flash of lightning. Two men, Moses and Elijah, appeared in glorious splendor, talking with Jesus. They spoke about his departure, which he was about to bring to fulfillment at Jerusalem. Peter and his companions were very sleepy, but when they became fully awake, they saw his glory and the two men standing with him. As the men were leaving Jesus, Peter said to him, "Master, it is good for us to be here. Let us put up three shelters—one for you, one for Moses and one for Elijah." (He did not know what his was saying.)

While he was speaking, a cloud appeared and enveloped them, and they were afraid as they entered the cloud. A voice came from the cloud, saying, "This is my Son, whom I have chosen; listen to him." When the voice had spoken, they found that Jesus was alone. The disciples kept this to themselves, and told no one at that time what they had seen. Luke 9:28-36

Jesus did more than share a significant insight here, He shared an experience they would never forget. Although we might first say the comparison is absurd, let us not forget the principle is the same. He was so believing and committed to these three apostles that He took the time to share a wonderful experience. They then became the inner circle of His apostles and ultimately the key leaders of the early church. The question we need to ask ourselves is this: "Are we spending quality time with our subordinates?"

I had a young executive come to me and ask if he could take a half hour of my time to discuss management principles. He then told me that over a two-year period he had watched me make decisions and set the company's direction, taking it to where it was today.

"How did you get that kind of wisdom?" he asked.

My first reaction was to thank him for the compliment, but as I thought about his first question I began to understand that the wisdom and experiences acquired over twenty-five years were valuable—maybe more valuable to this young executive than to me. Not to give away what I had learned would be a sin.

I went home that night thinking what a tremendous responsibility and a great privilege goes with leadership. I have years of experience—some successes and unfortunately some failures. I have a responsibility to the people who are working with me to spend quality time training them. That way, maybe they can avoid some of my past mistakes.

In today's marketplace it is unfortunate that those who do have wisdom to pass on are either too busy or not interested in sharing their experiences. We must remember that training just one person is very significant. It's like dropping a pebble in the pond: the ripples will affect many. Great leaders should always

Another method of Jesus' teaching and training the Apostles was spending quality time with His people

15

be building great leaders. The only way that this can be realized is by leaders spending quality time with their associates—the kind of quality time Jesus spent with His apostles.

4. Commitment and Perseverance

Jesus was not to be denied. He knew His mission and He was committed to the end, even understanding the price was the cross. His role model of sacrificial commitment must have been a tremendous inspiration to His disciples.

I believe Jesus was aware that not everyone was willing to make the sacrifice to be a follower. In Luke 14, He challenges prospective followers to consider the cost before signing on:

> *If anyone comes to me and does not hate his father and mother, his wife and children, his brothers and sisters—yes, even his own life—he cannot be my disciple. And anyone who does not carry his cross and follow me cannot be my disciple.* Luke 14:26-27

I believe the same applies to us today as leaders. There is a cost to be paid in any leadership capacity. Great leaders will model that trait. Ultimately a leader's ability to demonstrate commitment will be evaluated by his or her associates and reflected in their desire to follow.

I love the commitment demonstrated by Jesus in Luke 9:

> *Jesus strictly warned them not to tell this to anyone. And he said, "The Son of Man must suffer many things and be rejected by the elders, chief priests and teachers of the law, and he must be killed and on the third day be raised to life."*

> *Then he said to them all: "If anyone would come after me, he must deny himself and take up his cross daily and follow me. For whoever wants to save his life will lose it, but whoever loses his life for me will save it. What good is it for a man to gain the whole world, and yet lose or forfeit his very self? If anyone is ashamed of me and my words, the Son of Man will be ashamed of him when he comes in his glory and in the glory of the Father and of the holy angels. I tell you the truth, some who are standing here will not taste death before they see the kingdom of*

> Ultimately, a leader's ability to demonstrate commitment will be evaluated by his or her associates and reflected in their desire to follow.

God." Luke 9:21-27

Don't you enjoy watching people who are dedicated to their work? That kind of perseverance separates the strong leaders from the weak ones. Today our company has 160-plus store managers and I've had the wonderful opportunity of watching them demonstrate a commitment to accomplishing their goals.

It's exciting for me to see how our management's competitiveness drives them to achieve their highest potential. When people ask me why Helzberg Diamonds is so successful in the jewelry industry, my answer is always the same: It's our great people and their desire to succeed that makes us the best we can be.

I always have to remind myself and our management people that it's easy to be a leader when things are going well. It's when our company hits a bump in the road that our leadership abilities are challenged.

Indeed, it's hard times that challenge us to take advantage of the greatest opportunity to be a role model of commitment and perseverance. That is when our associates are going to look to us to see what we are really made of. It is in those times that we can reflect the real spirit of Jesus Christ.

I remember one summer when my son Ryan was playing Little League baseball. He was the catcher and a pretty good one. But as a hitter, he was mediocre. To make it worse, he was in a slump. For five games he went hitless and only occasionally reached a base on balls. He was depressed.

One day after a game he told me he wanted to quit. The humiliation was apparently too much. I wouldn't let him quit, so I shared my "quitter story" with him.

"There are two reasons you can't quit," I said. "First, you made a commitment at the beginning of the season to be the team's catcher. You need to finish that commitment. Second, if you quit when times are tough, you will find it easier to quit

Chapter One

when obstacles are in your way. Instead, you should try reaching down and finding the conviction and courage to get through. Don't take the easy way out, son. Let's finish the final two games of the season."

"OK," Ryan said, somewhat uncertainly. "If you say so."

I called Ryan's coach that night and told him about our conversation. He responded by taking Ryan to the batting cage the next night and suggesting a few improvements in his technique. The next game Ryan was hitless in his first two at-bats. In the bottom of the last inning he came up to bat with his team trailing by one run with two outs and a man on second base.

I was petrified. Ryan walked to the plate and took his stance. On the very first pitch he made contact. The ball lifted over the pitcher's head, over the center fielder's head, and finally over the fence! It landed in the parking lot. Ryan's first hit in five games was a home run! His team won the game. On the way home Ryan looked over at me and said, "Dad, if I ever want to quit again, tell me the 'quitter story.'"

To me, a quitter is also a leader who takes the easy way out—focusing on the short term when faced with strategic dilemmas.

Immediate profits have replaced investment in the long-term health of many companies. You've probably seen leaders who have taken the easy road and suffered the inevitable poor results for their organizations in the long term.

Through the years, many businesses have had to deal with unfortunate publicity. In those incredibly difficult times, it is leadership alone that can salvage a reputation. When Johnson & Johnson faced the tremendous Tylenol scare several years back, the company made a courageous decision by pulling the product off retail shelves and making the statement that consumers must be protected at all costs. This has to rank as one of the more fearless business decisions of all time. The quick action on the part of Johnson & Johnson was not lost on American consumers, many of whom stayed loyal to the product and still swear by it today.

On the flip side, we all know stories about corporations that have closed their doors due to cowardly decisions on the part of management.

People often ask me how I get through difficult times and still maintain the kind of commitment Christ would want me to have. My answer is always the same: It's because of my relationship with Christ, my wife Martha, and my close friends.

Only Jesus can give us the inner strength we need. I have experienced His presence so many times in my life during troubled times, and I'm not sure I would have survived without Him.

And I thank God for my wife and friends who have kept me committed to my mission. They're always there to remind me of the "quitter story," whenever I need to hear it.

I think people want actions, not words. Jesus backed up His challenge to commitment by giving His life. With that dedication, wouldn't you have followed Jesus? Do our associates see that kind of perseverance in us? Are we prepared to pay the price in our organizations during the difficult times?

5. Fair and Equitable Evaluation

Jesus was fair and equitable in His evaluation of people. Throughout the Gospels Jesus demonstrated a consistency when complimenting, challenging, or admonishing those who surrounded Him. He was consistent in his business management, an outstanding trait of a leader.

Jesus' fair and equitable treatment of people was probably most clearly evidenced in His dealings with the Pharisees. This sect of religious zealots, who perverted God's laws, began the movement to send Jesus to the cross. Jesus remained steadfast in publicly condemning the Pharisees. Consistently throughout the Gospels, Jesus points out the Pharisees' sin in situation after situation. One of these classic confrontations occurred in the synagogue, as described in Luke:

On a Sabbath Jesus was teaching in one of the synagogues, and a woman was there who had been crippled by a spirit for

> Jesus backed up His challenge to commitment by giving His life. Are we prepared to pay the price in our organizations during the difficult times?

eighteen years. She was bent over and could not straighten up at all. When Jesus saw her, he called her forward and said to her, "Woman, you are set free from your infirmity." Then he put his hands on her, and immediately she straightened up and praised God.

Indignant because Jesus had healed on the Sabbath, the synagogue ruler said to the people, "There are six days for work. So come and be healed on those days, not on the Sabbath."

The Lord answered him, "You hypocrites! Doesn't each of you on the Sabbath untie his ox or donkey from the stall and lead it out to give it water? Then should not this woman, a daughter of Abraham, whom Satan has kept bound for eighteen long years, be set free on the Sabbath day from what bound her?" Luke 13:10-16

And again in Luke, chapter 12, Jesus finishes telling His apostles a parable about fairness and how we will be judged. This scripture is an excellent example of Jesus' fair and equitable leadership. He says,

The servant who knows his master's will and does not get ready or does not do what his master wants will be beaten with many blows. But the one who does not know and does things deserving punishment will be beaten with few blows. From everyone who has been given much, much will be demanded; and from the one who has been entrusted with much, much more will be asked. Luke 12:47-48

Even the Apostles were unsure about their place in God's kingdom as Jesus described it. Peter exclaimed that the Apostles had given up their homes to follow Him. Jesus' reply revealed His idea of fair and equitable:

"I tell you the truth," Jesus said to them, "no one who has left home or wife or brothers or parents or children for the sake of the kingdom of God will fail to receive many times as much in this age and, in the age to come, eternal life." Luke 18:29-30

Probably never before in the history of our free enterprise system has there been more need to spend quality time with associates. Motivating and managing people through career planning, as well as offering timely appraisals and honest evaluations, are needed in every organization. I am amazed at how many organizations still do not take human resource management seriously. And how many companies don't have the proper tools for hiring, training, and evaluating their people?

At Helzberg Diamonds I have had the privilege to see our human resource management mature, and I've witnessed the impact of this strategy with people at all levels of the organization. Good human resource management can be an outstanding and motivating strategy. Our associates look forward to their evaluation because they know it is a great opportunity to discuss their strengths and weaknesses.

As Christian leaders in the marketplace, we need to encourage the evaluation process. Our associates deserve to know when they have excelled and when they have not realized their true potential. Most of all, they need to know we care.

As Christians, we sometimes tend to believe our compassion should overrule the need for telling the truth as we see it. However, I think Jesus' definition of compassion would be a "fair and equitable" evaluation of what the person is bringing to the company or organization.

I believe the bedrock of good human resource leadership is management by objective with an evaluation of associate accomplishments. To do this, we need to:

• Agree with an associate on what is to be accomplished within a set time frame.

• Offer an intermediate evaluation of the associate's progress and ensure that resources are available for his or her accomplishment.

• Conclude with a final review and appropriate reward for success.

These three basic steps are fundamental to an organization's success. In our business we have even found that intermediate reviews of goal accomplishments should include financial compensation in the form of commissions and bonuses.

> Probably never before in the history of our free enterprise system has there been more need to spend quality time with associates.

Chapter One

Helzberg Diamonds has a disciplined process for hiring, training, motivating, evaluating, and career planning. That orderly progression is necessary for me to know the assets of our people and, more importantly, it lets them know what they have to offer the company.

Most "for-profit" organizations have some form of this evaluation process. It's the non-profit and Christian organizations that tend to think this procedure isn't needed. Some organizations believe that it's "unspiritual" to tell people they are not doing their jobs right. They seem to believe that if these persons (who are, in fact, employees of the non-profit organization) are called by God, we should not interfere with their poor performance. That, in my opinion, is absolutely wrong.

We forget several important facts by adopting this sort of silence. If people are not doing the job, they probably know it. If they are failing, the rest of the organization can probably see it. By not acting, we are saying it is OK for the organization to fail. And finally, if we don't act, mediocrity will overtake the organization and become its standard.

I believe Christ's way would be to confront such people honestly and openly. Evaluate the person and point out the deficiencies and develop a plan to correct them. If employees are simply misplaced or they don't have the gifts and abilities for the job, tell them. Let them move on so that the organization may move ahead as well. Both will be better off in the long run.

As I read through Luke and see how Jesus dealt with His disciples, I believe He evaluated them consistently and fairly. Jesus was the first world-class equal opportunity employer. His apostles always knew where they were in their relationship with Him. This is mandatory if we are to have good productivity and healthy employee relationships.

6. Standards and Ethics

Jesus lived the perfect ethical life. Time and time again His standards were challenged as in Luke 4, when Satan tempted Him three times:

The devil said to him, "If you are the Son of God, tell this stone to become bread."

Jesus answered, "It is written: 'Man does not live on bread alone.'"

The devil led him up to a high place and showed him in an instant all the kingdoms of the world. And he said to him, "I will give you all their authority and splendor, for it has been given to me, and I can give it to anyone I want to. So if you worship me, it will all be yours."

Jesus answered, "It is written: 'Worship the Lord your God and serve him only.'"

The devil led him to Jerusalem and had him stand on the highest point of the temple. "If you are the Son of God," he said, "throw yourself down from here. For it is written:

'He will command his angels concerning you to guard you carefully; they will lift you up in their hands, so that you will not strike your foot against a stone.'"

Jesus answered, "It says: 'Do not put the Lord your God to the test.'"

When the devil had finished all this tempting, he left him until an opportune time.

Luke 4:3-13

Jesus was simply saying, "I will not forfeit God's ways." Today many of our free enterprise leaders are engaging in practices I'm sure Jesus would say are unethical. As Christian leaders we must know and exercise the ethics that Christ would demand, with no compromises.

Probably the single biggest negative factor affecting our free enterprise system today is the ethical vacuum. There are so many examples from the last decade. The investment banking industry, for instance, crippled our system with junk bonds, and the hostile takeover damage is still not totaled. The temptation to take the greedy way led many companies into destructive debt and, far too often, bankruptcy. Companies were destroyed, and

> Jesus was the first world-class equal opportunity employer.

Chapter One

people's lives were turned upside down.

Unethical business practices recorded over the past decade remain at an all time high. As I read *The Wall Street Journal,* I have to ask if a business can be successful and ethical at the same time.

Some of the greatest challenges in life can arise when one's ethics are tested. When tempted by egos or monetary desires to do that which Jesus would not approve of, we have an opportunity to stand in the gap for Him. We have an opportunity to make a decision that Christ would want rather than what the world desires. It is during these times when the people who work for us and with us will be looking to us for the great leadership and moral convictions that are Christ's standards.

The single biggest negative factor affecting our free enterprise system today is the ethical vacuum.

As leaders in the free enterprise system, we will be tempted to make decisions for personal gain, short-term profit, or maybe just plain ego. We have the opportunity to say "yes" or "no."

Looking at Helzberg Diamonds, I would have to say our strongest heritage is that we try to operate our business with a high degree of ethics. I believe our people see that, understand it, and as a result are encouraged to live up to that morally correct spirit themselves.

When I travel the country talking to our associates I find that the thing they seem most proud of is our company's character. As one twenty-five-year-old store manager told me, "Any company can offer pretty merchandise and beautiful catalogues, but it takes a special business to do it all with integrity and character. It feels good to be part of that."

As chief executive officer of Helzberg Diamonds, I am very proud of that statement. I believe that God honors integrity and character as much as our customers do.

Jesus began His earthly ministry in the power of the Holy Spirit. Through the fullness of the Holy Spirit and being obedient to God's word, He was able to overcome the temptations of Satan in the desert.

I believe we have to ask ourselves the serious question, "Are we allowing our ministry in life to be empowered by the Holy Spirit?" Or have we allowed Satan to entice us with personal gains and pleasures that are, in effect, diminishing our ability to minister for Christ?

God uses temptation in our lives to strengthen us and to show others what He looks like through us. We should be challenged to be the person God has called us to be—today, tomorrow, and forever.

7. Servant Leader

Jesus looked at Himself as a servant of the people. Although the Bible reveals Jesus as the Son of God, Jesus himself pointed out that He was a servant. This is a difficult concept for many to accept. But in Luke 22 He says it so well, after watching His apostles squabble over who was best:

They began to question among themselves which of them it might be who would do this.

Also a dispute arose among them as to which of them was considered to be greatest. Jesus said to them, "The kings of the Gentiles lord it over them; and those who exercise authority over them call themselves Benefactors. But you are not to be like that. Instead, the greatest among you should be like the youngest, and the one who rules like the one who serves. For who is greater, the one who is at the table or the one who serves? But I am among you as one who serves. You are those who have stood by me in my trials. And I confer on you a kingdom, just as my Father conferred one on me, so that you may eat and drink at my table in my kingdom and sit on thrones, judging the twelve tribes of Israel." Luke 22:23-30

I believe this trait above all others exemplifies a great leader. Today many corporations and organizations are beginning to realize that the old traditional organization charts just will not work with the CEO at the top and the associates on the bottom. The interesting answer to this problem is to turn the chart upside down: Put the associates at the top with the CEO on the bottom.

A leader clearly seen as a person serving his or her associates through management style will be a leader held in high esteem long after a hard day's work.

Our egos sometimes get the best of us. As speakers we often want to be introduced with great fanfare. As the "author of many books," or voted "The Best" something or other. We are like roosters who think the sun has risen to hear them crow. That's not exactly how Jesus would have us think of ourselves, or how He thought of Himself.

In contrast we need to look at our jobs and think of the people working with us and remember that we need to be their servants so they can be better associates.

A leader clearly seen as a person serving his or her associates through management style will be a leader held in high esteem long after a hard day's work.

I struggle with this leadership trait because I have a big ego. God is teaching me, though. I am beginning to understand that power, titles, and status do not bring peace. Peace only comes when you find His grace; when you are where He wants you. Then it will follow that your actions are His commands.

Servant leadership can also include the technique of "how" we do our job. If you need a job done, it doesn't help to come across as dictatorial. You can state the task simply and clearly, without having to make your associates jump through hoops. A thoughtless word or action can be the beginning of the end in any relationship. Those who have a need to be harsh and unkind are not reflecting the servant leadership style of Jesus. If one is going to lead, then one must lead without emotional attachment to an overblown ego.

I usually try to start a management conversation by saying, "Let's work through this situation and find out how we can improve this." Then any suggestions or ideas I offer will usually be welcomed. Eventually this becomes our idea, not my idea. When the concept comes to fruition, we can all say we had a part in its inception.

Normally, the end result is ownership by associates. Not only is the task completed, but everyone feels good about the process and the outcome.

I know it can't be done every time and sometimes you just have to say, "Go do it." But if you have built a track record of showing concern for your associates, they will understand and give you the benefit of the doubt when decisions have to be made.

Running a business is like making bank deposits and withdrawals. If you are constantly making good deposits with your people, giving them a lot of entrepreneurial room to make decisions, they will respect that occasionally you have to make a withdrawal. That would be a situation where you have to say "Let's do it my way!"

My sole responsibility in our organization is to make sure our associates have the ability to close the sale with the customer. If I can do that with an economic frequency that's viable, I've served our associates, investors, and customers well.

Although "servant leadership" has been a buzzword for the last decade, few organizations really live it. Why? Because it takes time, patience, and trust. Christ lived it. He encourages us to do the same.

Can Jesus be a great role model when it comes to good leadership and management traits? I believe so. Our challenge is, "think management and leadership traits, then read the gospel of Luke." It may begin to change your management style.

Chapter One

1. Does my management style reflect the traits of Jesus Christ?

Objectively evaluate yourself. Rate yourself from 1 through 10, 1 being the lowest, and 10 being the highest rating. Then ask a colleague who knows you to evaluate you the same way. See how someone else perceives you and your performance. Compare the two and start the process of change where needed.

Rank 1 (low) through 10 (high) on each trait:

	LOW	HIGH
Mission With a Passion	1 2 3 4 5 6 7 8 9 10	

Do you know your mission in life?
Does your organization have a mission
statement?

	LOW	HIGH
Focus and Understanding	1 2 3 4 5 6 7 8 9 10	

Are you focused? Do your
associates have a clear idea
of what is expected of them?

	LOW	HIGH
Teacher and Trainer	1 2 3 4 5 6 7 8 9 10	

Do you spend quality time
teaching and training your
associates to become the quality
people you expect them to be?

	LOW	HIGH
Commitment and Perseverance	1 2 3 4 5 6 7 8 9 10	

How committed are you to your goals?
Do you have the kind of perseverance that
that Jesus would want you to have?

	LOW	HIGH
Fair and Equitable	1 2 3 4 5 6 7 8 9 10	

Are your consistently fair when
dealing with your associates?
Do they know what to expect from you?

	LOW	HIGH
Standards and Ethics	1 2 3 4 5 6 7 8 9 10	

Do you operate in business
with a high degree of ethics?
What is your motivation for success?

Servant Leader	1 2 3 4 5 6 7 8 9 10	

Do you put your ego last and your
associates first? Are you serving your
company to the best of your ability?

2. How can I begin this week to look more like Jesus?

3. When will I read the Gospel of Luke?

SCRIPTURE REFERENCES

Luke 4:3-13   Luke 10:1-12

Luke 4:18-19   Luke 10:16

Luke 4:43   Luke 10:17

Luke 5:33-35, 37-39   Luke 12:47-48

Luke 8:10   Luke 13:10-16

Luke 9:1-6   Luke 14:26-27

Luke 9:21-27   Luke 18:29-30

Luke 9:28-36   Luke 22:23-30

Chapter Two

THE BOTTOM LINE

S everal years ago the chief executive of a major national retailer and his executive assistant were interviewing me over dinner at New York's Pierre Hotel. I was finishing my second cup of coffee when the CEO gave me a piercing look. "What are the priorities in your life, Jeff? What makes you tick?"

No one had ever asked me those questions before, and it took me by surprise. I had never really taken the time to verbalize my priorities, but I told the CEO they were really very simple: faith, family, friends, and career.

"You know what's interesting?" I added. "When I get those priorities confused and my job becomes number one, I find myself very quickly becoming a less productive and unfocused executive. On the other hand, when my priorities are in order, I feel I'm at my best."

A couple of days later I was talking to the CEO's assistant who was at the interview.

"Did I shoot myself in the foot with my response to your boss's questions?" I asked.

How do we measure up to God's priorities?

Are we over-achievers, underachievers, or God's achievers?

Chapter Two

"No, you sure didn't," he said. "I know he appreciated your honesty."

I was glad to hear that, because I'd given the only answer I could. I'd made up my mind that I wouldn't work in an environment where I couldn't set my own priorities. Faith, family, friends, and career are important to me, in that order. However, there are times when one of these priorities might be more vital than the others.

 For example, when I started my new job at Helzberg Diamonds, I spent a large part of my life getting acclimated to the company's needs and, in turn, letting the company get to know me. Over the last few years, I've put in an unusual amount of time and energy building the business. This often requires more hours away from home, but my family understands, once I explain the situation. Likewise, I made sure that I devoted all the time necessary to my family during those tough times when I was needed most. I still did my job to the best of my ability, but I didn't take on any special assignments and I explained the circumstances to my boss.

Spending significant amounts of time with loved ones is important, but whatever the amount, make sure it is quality time. I think we need to look at priorities as a state of mind. I may spend eight hours at work today and only half an hour with my son Ryan, but based on the quality and compassion of the time I spend with him, both Ryan and I will know what my real priorities are.

In fact, every time I think about priorities, I'm reminded of the time when Ryan played his first Little League game. I remember it well. He was only nine years old then, and he was coming back to the bench midway through the first inning. His hat was crooked, his pants were sloppy, his socks were hanging down—he was the picture of a kid who looked like he didn't have his priorities together. Well, I was about five minutes late to the game, so I slid up to the back of the bench and asked Ryan what the score was.

"Thirteen to nothing," he said.

"Thirteen to nothing?!" I yelped, in a loud voice that could be heard all the way to the bleachers.

Ryan eyed me calmly. "It's OK, Dad. We haven't come up to bat yet."

He had his priorities in order. It was good old Dad who was confused.

I think a lot of people don't understand what their priorities are. The marketplace looks for people who are committed to their organizations, to one another, and who are dedicated to the spirit of what that organization is doing. It's our obligation and our responsibility to combine these priorities with God's priorities: what He would have us do in our lives.

To be an effective business executive, one has to focus on a basic list of priorities for the long haul. That's exactly the point I was making during that job interview. To my surprise I stayed in the running for the job until the last cut, when they finally went with a guy from inside their own company. However, that whole episode made it very clear to me how essential it is for people, especially Christians, to establish the focus that will determine how they spend their time and energy in the marketplace.

Ask yourself these questions: *What am I living for? What is important to me? Am I working on the right things in my life?* If you really believe you have been called by God to the marketplace, then that is your mission field, and you need to be just as serious in your mission as the person who goes to Africa or China to serve Jesus Christ.

The first thing the marketplace identifies with is people who are committed to their jobs, companies, and associates, and who want to be successful. Over the years I have found these kinds of persons exciting to be around. They are dynamic in their nature and have a strong desire for achievement. Combine these traits with the dynamics of knowing Jesus Christ and wanting to fulfill His sovereign plan, and you have the total business person God has really called us to be.

Chapter Two

Unfortunately, too many Christians in the marketplace today are either speeding along out of control or limping along on half their cylinders. From my observations, I believe Christians fall into three groups: Overachievers, Underachievers, and God's achievers

OVERACHIEVERS

Overachievers have several things in common:

- They are frequently consumed by their careers.
- They never seem to have time for their families.
- They have a strong desire for titles and material possessions.
- They believe the business can't survive without them.

People who are often consumed by their jobs feel they must work almost every day. They let the real priorities suffer while they race to "get ahead." These men and women also share other traits. They find it hard to take a break, and, if the business is open, they feel compelled to be there. Indeed, they allow themselves little freedom to miss any time from work.

On the Friday of the first week of my new job as president of Helzberg Diamonds, my associates hailed me as I walked out the door.

"See you tomorrow morning," they said. I was surprised to find out they were expected to be at their desks on Saturday.

As the president, I didn't quite understand why they would all be working on Saturday, so I showed up unannounced to find them all sitting around the office, doing almost everything except work. When I asked them why they were there, the only reply was that they had always worked on Saturdays. It was a carryover from another era.

That idea certainly didn't jibe with my own philosophy, which is to get the job done in the prescribed time, then take a few days off with the family, pursuing other interests. "Work if you need to work," I told them, "but don't feel like you have to be here six days a week, month after month. I want you to give a fair share of hours to the company, but leave time to be with

> Too many Christians in the marketplace today are either speeding along out of control or limping along on half their cylinders.

your spouses and families."

I went on to explain that weekend work at the office should only be for special projects and handling the seasonal fluctuations that drive our retail business. Their response was surprise and relief that they could feel free to enjoy their weekends. Retailing can be a very demanding profession. It is my job as C.E.O. of the company to be the role model for balance. I feel this stability is not only important for our general office associates but for our store associates as well. While most of our retail personnel work Saturday and/or Sunday, we encourage them to take two days off during the week to relax and have some family time.

In fact, the *lack of family time* is another common characteristic of the overachiever. Closely related to workaholics, these people constantly toil at the job, often excluding the valuable hours necessary to be with their families. Even office equipment, such as phone mail, becomes addictive for such people, who use the system to stay in control of work. In reality, these devices can begin to control us, if we let them.

Those quality moments spent with children are of the utmost importance. For example, our daughter recently graduated from high school and was looking forward to her field hockey scholarship at the College of William and Mary. While Kristen was in high school, my wife and I had the opportunity to host seventy-five young ladies from different parts of the country, all field hockey players, for a dinner in our home.

It seemed like just a few days ago when we arrived in Kansas City and our little freshman daughter was nervous about being the new kid in school without any friends. Now here she was an accomplished athlete, at home with new friends from all over the country and on her way to college. Seeing our daughter in this setting made us thankful for the times we've been able to spend with her.

So, I encourage you to spend time with your loved ones. Remember that kids grow up fast. Don't wake up and find your children have grown up without you.

Aside from overlooking some of life's best moments, over-

Chapter Two

achievers also have *a strong desire for titles and material possessions.* They think about what they don't have rather than what they do have. Those who are rich in spirit are always prosperous, no matter how much money they make, while those who are poor in spirit are truly impoverished, despite their money. Overachievers' identities are wrapped up in the positions they hold, in the type of car they drive, or where they live. Achieving one level only increases the desire to go on to the next level. Having a nice car is no longer enough—they must have a car that no one else has. They demand a bigger house to prove they have achieved the proper social status.

I'd like to underscore the fact that there is nothing wrong with having a title, a nice car, or a beautiful house. My wife and I live in a lovely home, and we both feel it is appropriate for both my corporate and community responsibilities. It's the *motive* for having these material possessions that has to be carefully considered. For me this is sometimes a tough reality check. I have to ask myself if what I want is appropriate. Does it provide balance in my life? If the answer is yes, then I feel OK about myself.

Another difficult thing for overachievers to realize is that the business can survive without them! They are absolutely convinced the company needs them for every decision and find it hard to delegate authority to anyone else.

Overachievers who believe they are that important to the business have done an injustice to the company by not providing the leadership needed by their associates. If no one can make decisions without your input, it will be difficult for your firm to survive. Remember, you may just not live forever!

Most overachievers will tell you that they love what they are doing. That may be, but it's also important to be true to yourself. Are you becoming one-dimensional, or are you doing what God would have you do?

At the age of fifty-five, a good friend of mine thought he had accomplished it all. He had a thriving brokerage practice, a beautiful home in Philadelphia, and a summer home at the shore. He also belonged to a fine country club and had a good reputation in the business community. In addition he was a prominent member in the Christian community, had been an elder in his church, and was on a couple of national Christian boards.

Outwardly he seemed to be a marvelous example of a successful person. Inwardly, his family life was dying a slow death. His relationship with his wife was strained to the point where she was contemplating divorce. His oldest son had been involved in drugs and dropped out of college. His daughter had become aloof to the family and had no relationship with her father.

Although he was a very busy and successful man, he never asked himself: *What does God call success?*

Yes, he worked sixty hours a week. And no, he didn't have time enough to spend with his wife. He missed the soccer games with his son, and never attended his daughter's ballet recitals.

I'll never forget the morning when my friend called me and told me he was waking up to the fact that he was living life for all the wrong reasons.

"This morning when I looked in the mirror, I saw a tired, lonely individual who was in desperate need of discovering real success . . . Christ-like success," he told me.

I knew what my friend meant. It's important to understand what God wants you to do with your life, and then maximize the potential of attaining those goals. So often this significant accomplishment may seem different from what the world calls success.

I've met people who thought just being busy meant being successful. It doesn't matter whether you are on the bottom rung of the career ladder or at the top. You can still allow yourself to be driven by that inner voice that says you aren't good enough, you aren't smart enough, unless you prove yourself in the eyes of the world.

Chapter Two

Having achieved worldly success doesn't necessarily make you an overachiever. You can be an overachiever and still lack wealth and abundance in your life.

We are on a constant treadmill. Our jobs—our careers—our extracurricular activities—will consume us if we allow them full reign. In today's competitive environment, companies expect more from us and the demands continue to increase. We have to take a stand on how much of ourselves we can give.

Our careers... our extra- curricular activities... will consume us if we allow them full reign.

To be an overachiever may mean you'll be a success in the eyes of others. Yet it is more important in the long run to be a success in the eyes of God. Becoming aware of God in one's life means truly realizing that God is part of everything we do. This is the antidote to mindless overachieving: understanding that God truly wants us to grow and accomplish His plan.

UNDERACHIEVERS

Like overachievers, underachievers also have some distinct traits:

- They feel becoming a Christian exempts them from hard work.

- They have no motivation, no drive to excel in the marketplace.

- They absolutely do not know how to enjoy life.

- They get wrapped up in their spiritual experience, lose their passion for career, and misinterpret the fact that Jesus wants us to be in the real world.

Underachievers are those I call lazy Christians. I have to admit these people get no sympathy from me. They have no work ethic. They demonstrate no desire to succeed or see their company be successful. In fact, they think it is somehow unspiritual to even mention success, let alone try to achieve it. Legitimate concern about becoming a workaholic turns into failure to put their efforts into a good day's work. For those who live this way, it is difficult to see Christ in their lives.

When I see people like this representing Christ, all I can do is lower my head in shame. As Christians we should be the most sensitive to doing our best, since everything we do is suppose to be "as unto the Lord." I don't think our performance on the job should be any different. Anything less than our best effort dishonors God.

I once had a store manager about whom people were saying, "He used to be a terrific manager, then he became a Christian!" I asked one of our executives to tell me the story behind this statement. He told me that the man had been one of our best store managers. He was highly productive, a great motivator, and his store always performed well.

"Then he became one of those 'born-again guys,'" the executive said, "and ever since then, he lost all his motivation."

I knew I had a mission. I had to meet this person. So, I bought a plane ticket that very day and flew out to meet him. Over a cup of coffee and conversation we talked about his store and its lack of productivity. Then I casually mentioned that I had learned he'd recently become a Christian.

He seemed to be blown away by this remark. He said to me excitedly, "I sure did! How did you know?"

I told him how people were beginning to compare his lackluster performance to his newfound Christian faith. I surprised him when I mentioned how embarrassed I was that he, as a Christian, had so little desire for success. I told him that in my opinion he was a poor witness to all of those watching his store's performance.

"Why would they want to become like you?" I asked.

That conversation opened some real avenues for discussion. We talked about his responsibility as a steward of the gifts God had given him and the poor role model he had become. We talked about commitment to Christ and how that related to his work experience. He had some great questions and I literally could see the fire return to his eyes as that old competitive desire began to return with a new purpose

Chapter Two

There's a great conclusion to this story and it's very simple. Twelve months after that cup of coffee this same store manager was one of the best performing store managers in the company. Month after month his store broke all kinds of records.

Did it affect his relationship with Jesus Christ positively? I think so.

Did it affect his ability to witness to people around him? I know so!

Now people have a high regard for his ability as a businessman and no longer label him as a "Christian underachiever." Now he is talked about as a guy with a great new desire to be successful, with his career, his family, and his faith.

In writing to the believers at Colosse, the Apostle Paul clearly addresses the issue of responsibility in performing our duties:

Let the word of Christ dwell in you richly as you teach and admonish one another with all wisdom, and as you sing psalms, hymns and spiritual songs with gratitude in your hearts to God. And whatever you do, whether in word or deed, do it all in the name of the Lord Jesus, giving thanks to God the Father through him. Colossians 3:16-17

And again:

Whatever you do, work at it with all your heart, as working for the Lord, not for men, since you know that you will receive an inheritance from the Lord as a reward. It is the Lord Christ you are serving. Colossians 3:23-24

These passages are all-inclusive regarding our responsibility to give our best performance, regardless of the circumstances. No distinction between secular employment and full-time ministry is mentioned.

GOD'S ACHIEVERS

God's achievers also have some very distinct traits

* They take Scripture seriously as a challenge.
* They strive for balance in their lives.
* They have a plan for accomplishment.
* They understand what sharing the Gospel
  really looks like.

Further, God's achievers live their lives based on the truth:

I urge you, brothers, in view of God's mercy, to offer your bodies as living sacrifices, holy and pleasing to God—this is your spiritual act of worship. Do not conform any longer to the pattern of this world, but be transformed by the renewing of your mind. Then you will be able to test and approve what God's will is—his good, pleasing and perfect will. Romans 12:1-2

These people seek to honor Christ and serve Him right where they are. They are developing a lifestyle distinct from the world.

God's achievers strive for balance. They avoid becoming overachievers and they are dismayed by underachievers. They blend their commitment to Jesus Christ, and everything He stands for, with a genuine responsibility to their business and the people in it.

Life doesn't happen by chance for God's achievers. They have a plan and a discipline through His grace. Three things are essential in the plan:

1. Creating goals that reflect a balanced life. You need to plan around your ambitions. How much time can you give to your career and your family? What about spiritual needs—your walk with Jesus Christ? All of those demands must be evaluated and then flexible goals established.

2. Holding yourself accountable to your goals. Search out people who will ask you hard questions and who are not afraid to tell you the truth. Your spouse could be one of those people. So can a close friend of the same sex with whom you easily relate. (Besides my wife, I have two men who hold me accountable to my beliefs on a regular basis.)

Chapter Two

When a person attains success by the world's yardstick, and does it with high moral and ethical standards, the impact on others becomes significant.

3. Developing a strong prayer life. I am convinced that without significant prayer you will not have the strength and grace to accomplish any of your long-term goals. Priorities will become confused and direction will be lost.

I also believe that, as God's achievers, He has called us to be people that model His ethical and professional standards in our work environment. As God's achievers we should conduct our business with the highest ethical standards. The kind of success and achievement we see in today's marketplace is often corrupted with a lack of integrity and moral business practice. But when a person attains success by the world's yardstick and does it with high moral and ethical standards, the impact on the people around him or her becomes significant.

God's achievers must also understand what sharing their faith really means. I don't believe most Christians know how to be really effective in sharing their love for Christ. We've been taught that witnessing means verbally sharing the Gospel. And when we read Matthew 5 and discover for ourselves that we are to be "the salt and light," our first thought should be: Am I living the gospel for my associates?

You are the salt of the earth. But if the salt loses its saltiness, how can it be made salty again? It is no longer good for anything, except to be thrown out and trampled by men.

You are the light of the world. A city on a hill cannot be hidden. Neither do people light a lamp and put it under a bowl. Instead they put it on its stand, and it gives light to everyone in the house. In the same way, let your light shine before men, that they may see your good deeds and praise your Father in heaven. Matthew 5:13-16

Do people understand your faith? There are times when we do need to tell people how to accept Christ, but most of us have a far greater impact with our actions rather than our words. I don't believe sharing the Gospel is an either/or proposition. We need to blend our actions with our words in fleshing out the gospel before the secular world.

When the famous missionary E. Stanley Jones asked Gandhi how to become a better missionary, Gandhi said, "Become more

42

like the man you claim you follow."

In my own life I have come to recognize the greatest sharing of my faith is through high business standards coupled with the integrity that I can project to the people around me. It doesn't take long, especially if you have management responsibility, for people around you to understand the basis of your faith. As Christians we need to spend less time talking about our faith and more time demonstrating we are the kind of people God wants us to be. That can be done best by demonstrating our beliefs through our priorities and our actions.

As God's achievers we should never forget that part of our responsibility is to be effective stewards of our time, our wisdom, our logic, our physical capabilities, and our financial resources.

We should exploit our God-given gifts every day. We should demonstrate that our drive to be successful is not for greed or personal interest, but to honor Christ. When that can be accomplished with integrity and the highest ethical business standards, we will have earned the recognition and credibility that will cause others to listen to us.

I am convinced that when I see Jesus face to face, He's not going to ask me specifically how many times I shared the gospel, how many talks I made, or how many books I wrote. Instead I think He'll say, "Jeff, did you live your life, hour by hour, day by day, so that all of the people I placed around you had an opportunity to see Me in you?"

How do we reflect the personality of Jesus Christ in our priorities, in our day-to-day activities in the marketplace? I believe that by setting an example as Jesus would have you do in your day-to-day living, you can reach your spiritual goals. That, in truth, is the real "bottom line."

Chapter Two

1. Where would my life be balanced on this scale? Where would I honestly have to rank myself?

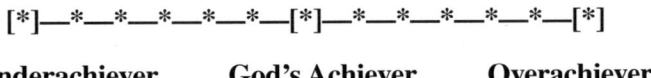

Underachiever   God's Achiever   Overachiever

2. Am I willing to ask a good Christian friend how he or she perceives my position on the scale?

3. If I'm not happy with my current position, what do I have to do to change?

4. Is it time to set some personal goals for my life?

5. How do I know I'm getting closer to where God wants me?

SCRIPTURE REFERENCES

Colossians 3:16-17
Colossians 3:23-24
Romans 12:1-2
Matthew 5:13-16

Chapter Three

ETHICS AND THE BALANCE SHEET

T he ugly side of humanity can always be found in national
    tabloids that grab our attention with sensational and
    provocative stories. Yet, in recent years, I've found stories
about unethical practices spilling out between the pages of prestigious publications like The Wall Street Journal. Headlines like
this blast the front pages, fueling the flame of discontent:

*"Junk King's Legacy"; "Shattered Family: Why Would Brothers
Who Had Everything Murder Their Parents?"; "Compulsive
Trading Brings Down Lawyer Who Used Client's Cash";
"Company Knew for Years Their Product Could Fail";
"Legislators Bouncing Checks Unprecedented."* The fact that
headlines like these are cropping up in century-old prestigious
publications like The Wall Street Journal is enough to make you sit
up and take notice that something is seriously wrong with society.

The Wall Street Journal was once the newspaper that reported
the successes and failures of companies and the people who ran
them. Now the real news of business has been bumped from the
front page. Today's stories outline the greed, corruption, and lack
of character that saturate our free enterprise system.

How do
we apply
God's moral
and ethical
standards to
business?

Chapter Three

If *The Wall Street Journal* is the report card for this, then we are failing badly. Each morning when I pick up my paper and begin to thumb through the major articles of the day, I am reminded of the incredible moral breakdown in our marketplace. There are always new stories that profile individuals and companies who have profited through questionable or outright unethical dealings. Even religious organizations have not been exempt from corruption, suffering the same problems as their secular counterparts.

From the savings and loan scandals and greedy investment banking firms to unscrupulous members of the medical and/or legal professions and the routine world of manufacturing and retailing-no segment of our society seems to be immune. To compound the problem, our elected officials often play some part in these schemes.

These premeditated deeds are rooted in greed, power, and self-centeredness. While the guilty often suffer the legal and professional consequences, one can only wonder how they have adversely affected their associates, their shareholders, and the thousands of young executives looking for role models.

In the 1970s the integrity of our national leadership was questioned as never before. First Vietnam and then Watergate shook our elected officials all the way to the White House. The first major blow to our national conscience was struck.

In the 1980s the unbridled drive to obtain more and more possessions added pressure to people already strained physically and financially. The media fueled the need to challenge authority. Even the primary unit of society, *the family*, fell victim to the pressures of "alternative" lifestyles and the "freedom" to be ourselves.

The 1990s seem to be the decade of cynicism. Trust is at an all time low, with people only wanting to report bad news. To compound the problem, our free enterprise system is changing because of increased competition at home and abroad. There are incredible advances in communication, significant changes in consumer buying habits, and shrinking job opportunities through mergers, takeovers, and bankruptcies. The resulting uncertainty and lack of security is forcing people to think about their future. Will their jobs be there tomorrow? Who controls their future?

In that kind of environment, how is it possible to define integrity?

Today the free enterprise system still reflects the values and integrity of its participants, so we have to ask ourselves, who should bear the blame if something goes wrong? Who is responsible when moral integrity starts to decay?

I believe the culture of any enterprise starts with its leaders. People in key and influential positions in government, business, or the professions must be aware that the ethics and integrity of their organization starts with them.

As leadership changes within the free enterprise system, the personality of the organization changes with it. Within that personality lies the opportunity to create a level of expectation with regard to integrity and ethics. In other words, *as leadership goes, so goes the organization.*

If leadership is that important, how do you build the right ethics into your firm? How do you saturate every level of management with moral principles?

Over the years I have seen Christian ethics reinforced in my own life and institutionalized throughout an organization. I am convinced a business can take on the personality of a leader who wants to demonstrate integrity and moral values that are consistent with the teachings of Scripture.

> As leadership goes, so goes the organization.

Of course the first requirement is for the leader to have some sense of what scriptures say about integrity and morals. Several verses have had significance in my life over the years. The first place I go is to the Psalms, so I can hear David talking to the Lord. He is so real you almost step into his shoes and feel his pain and sense his desire to know God:

Vindicate me, O Lord, for I have led a blameless life; I have trusted in the Lord without wavering. Test me, O Lord, and try me, examine my heart and my mind; for your love is ever before me, and I walk continually in your truth. Psalms 26:1-3

Chapter Three

In reading this passage, I sense that David was trying to discipline his life to be a godly man and to live with the kind of integrity that would please the Lord.

When I get up each morning, I should say, "God, I know you are going to put some situations in front of me today where my character, my integrity, and everything else is going to be put on trial. Let me be like David and be burdened to walk in truth."

The book of Proverbs also has honor and principle stamped throughout. To me this is what God's integrity looks like:

The man of integrity walks securely, but he who takes crooked paths will be found out. Proverbs 10:9

We may hide our lack of integrity for a while, but never from God, and never for long.

With all your burdens and pressures, have you ever felt insecure? A man of integrity is secure. The one who lacks integrity will be exposed. We may hide our lack of integrity for a while, but never from God, and never for long:

The righteous man leads a blameless life; blessed are his children after him. Proverbs 20:7

Our character has an impact on our children! A good name not only is to be honored, it brings blessings with it and provides a fine example for our children to follow and build on. How do you think the children of those guilty headline-makers feel about their parents? What kind of heritage do they have?

The Bible gives specific directions on how ethics and morals should permeate our lives. It is also clear that God will give us the strength and courage to be the people He wants us to be.

Making the transition from knowledge to practice is not always simple. In my experience three steps are essential if an individual or an organization wants to operate with integrity:

1. Write down what you stand for.

2. Live it out in all your actions.

3. Be accountable to others.

WRITE DOWN WHAT YOU STAND FOR

Ask yourself what you personally stand for, then write it down for all to see. Publicize it so your associates and customers can see who you really are. The greatest way in the world to promote integrity in our free enterprise system will be to get it out of the closet. In all aspects of our lives, it is amazing how much more direction we have when our guidelines and goals are in front of us. Integrity and character are not any different.

Ask yourself how this applies to your work environment. Whether you are the president of a company, have other leadership responsibilities, or just work in the marketplace where people depend on relationships, what you stand for is important to your associates.

There is something inherently good about taking the moral principles and integrity you stand for and incorporating them consistently into your policies and procedures. Everyone then can clearly see what you and your company stand for.

Many companies talk the game, but the principles they write on paper don't resemble their day-to-day actions in the marketplace.

Recently I was talking to a CEO of a large company who is highly respected by the business community and who I really think, in his heart, has the conviction to try and do what is right.

"Jeff," he said, "you reach a point out here in the free enterprise system where you've wallowed in the muck for so long you begin to lose perspective of what integrity and ethics are all about. If you steal pencils long enough, it probably won't be a big deal when you start stealing ink pens, and after that, it's pilfering personal computers."

I thought his was an interesting perspective and told him so. I also mentioned that I felt we needed to discipline ourselves to constantly think about what is right, why it's right, and what

Chapter Three

God would have us do. That's why writing down what you stand for in your own personal code of ethics is essential.

A code of ethics is not only important for companies to have, but it's something that you can use on a personal basis to measure the principles to which you adhere.

Writing down what you stand for in your own personal code of ethics is essential.

A code of ethics can also be the great rallying point for a company and one that creates pride in your associates. People want to know what their company stands for and for what they will be held accountable.

A code of ethics defines character and integrity. The rules are in print for everyone to see, and they apply to everyone in the organization, from the top to the bottom.

This kind of simple document can significantly reduce confusion and develop accountability for integrity within the total organization. The Helzberg Diamonds' code of ethics is not a static one; we refine and improve it annually. I have included it in the Appendix (page 145) as an example of how a business code of ethics might look.

This document is reviewed and signed by each associate in our company once a year. When situations arise where discipline is necessary, we review this document with the associates as a reminder that they have made these commitments to the company. As I like to say, it takes a lot of the mystery out of what we mean when we say "We want to run our company with character and integrity at all levels."

Our code of ethics serves as the bedrock for our decision making when it comes to discipline. It also protects the company when we must make the decision to terminate an associate for lack of integrity. Finally, as a business person who wants to represent Christ in the marketplace, it allows me to feel that I did everything I could to let our associates know our company's definition of integrity.

LIVE IT—IN ALL YOUR ACTIONS

Transforming a business into an ethical concern requires leaders who demonstrate that there will be no compromises when it comes to integrity. For example, it's easy to put out a policy memo that states how the organization is going to handle terms on invoices, but it's another thing to firmly act on that policy and pay the invoices on a timely basis, regardless of the business climate.

Several years ago I was a division president of a national retail company. The parent company was having serious cash flow problems and borrowed to the point of exceeding planned interest expenses. As a result of being nearly eaten alive by this financial obligation, the firm made a conscious decision to slow down payments to its resources. Obviously, this was a major violation of good business conduct.

Typically in business when a vendor sells merchandise to a retailer, he will offer a discount if the merchandise is paid for early or on a specific due date. For example, if merchandise is purchased from a vendor and the terms are 2 percent, the resource expects you to take your 2 percent discount. They also expect you to pay the bill in thirty days. We were being asked by our parent company to take the 2 percent, but pay the bill in sixty days. If the resource asked why payments were late, we were to explain it away as a "mistake."

There was no question that our parent company had made a serious error in violating the relationships we had with hundreds of resources. As the division president I had to tell our corporate parent that what it was doing was wrong. I knew that this viewpoint wouldn't be a popular one, and that I might suffer from the fallout. Yet I knew I couldn't ask my people to do something I personally felt was unprincipled and immoral.

As I look back, I can remember how tense it was at the time. The financial officer of the parent company and I butted heads. He accused me of insubordination, and several days of heated discussions followed, resulting in the subject being kicked all the way up to the chief executive officer.

Finally some sanity prevailed and I was told, discreetly, to do what I thought was right. I found out later most of the other major divisions ended up slowing down their payment terms. Your conclusion would probably be the same as mine: The company had made the same decision that many companies are making today—believing that profit pays more than integrity.

Three years later, that same company was put on a "credit check" by its vendors and six months later filed for Chapter 11. Due to the greed and irresponsible actions by the company leaders, it will probably never regain its respectability in the marketplace.

 Each difficult situation we face has to be thoroughly reviewed for its specific consequences. I would not begin to try and give an answer for each circumstance we might encounter, but I know in my heart if our focus is on Christ, He will give us the wisdom to do what's right. He will also give us the strength to accept the consequences, whatever they might be.

Perhaps you are thinking that your situation is different from mine and that you might be fired for speaking out. Well, in a sense I, too, was let go. Six months later I was told, "We're going to sell the business and you go with it. You aren't one of our team players."

Actions always speak louder than words. It's tragic that so many major American corporations give mixed signals by their often shady decisions that show little concern for customers, associates, or the company itself.

I believe many leaders feel these decisions have to be made for short-term reasons, but neglect the long-term consequences that affect their business as well as the entire industry.

People understand who we are by how we act. There is no stronger statement that defines us than the decisions we make each day. We either run our business with integrity or we don't. As the saying goes, *you can fool some of the people some of the time, but you can't fool all of the people all of the time.*

BE ACCOUNTABLE TO OTHERS

I find the first two points mentioned easy to talk about, but much harder to execute. To follow through with steps one and two, the most basic requirement needed is "accountability."

I know I personally need at least two or three people with whom I can develop a covenant relationship. These are persons I trust, who know me, who care about me, and upon whom I can depend. I rely on them to hold me accountable to the moral values by which I live my life. Whether you run a company or are the manager of a department, you're going to be under a great deal of pressure from time to time. And that's when people are going to lean on us to do the things we know we shouldn't be doing.

When I face that kind of situation, or when I am dealing with a problem where I need wise counsel, I pull in my covenant network of people who really care and whose clarity and moral sense I value. We all need those kinds of friends.

If you are married, the first member of your network should be your spouse. My wife Martha has been a great resource for me over the years. She will listen to me and then hold me accountable for my actions.

Also, I feel it's extremely important that members in your network are friends of the same gender. Accordingly, I have a couple of good friends who, no matter how difficult the situation, are willing to listen. Believe me, there have been many times when I have felt pressure that might have easily derailed my integrity and moral values.

Early in my career I was asked to reduce markdown dollars on the operating statement. The chief executive officer was insistent and applied every coercive tactic he could to get me to comply. I can still remember him saying, "Over the next six months you're going to have to figure out some clever accounting entries to make sure we're on our markdown plan."

At that point I began to justify reasons for not booking markdowns in the month they were taken. I had myself convinced after the first month that no damage would be done. Of course, after the second month the pressure just continued to build because we now had markdowns that were underaccrued from the previous month and markdowns that the CEO expected me not to book in the current month.

Our little game now had become a big game as the numbers increased each month. After the third month I became seriously concerned. I knew what we were doing wasn't right. I knew what we had done wasn't reflecting our true performance on the operating statement. I began to realize very clearly that this was affecting the value system of our entire company.

I didn't know which way to turn. The fiscal quarter end was in front of me. No matter what I did, I would betray someone. I realized a tremendous need to share this dilemma with my closest friend. His advice was essential to me.

> God will also hold us responsible for the gifts He has given us. "To whom much is given, much will be required."

Although he didn't come up with any exciting revelations, he did offer me great comfort and gave me back my courage and conviction. He validated what I knew I needed to do all along. He also told me that I would have someone praying for me every step of the way. That kind of friendship is precious and can't be measured on today's secular scale.

To be honest, I'm not sure what I would have done without those caring but firm words. That conversation gave me the courage to do what was right. I made the decision to book all the appropriate liabilities for the quarter. It's been situations like this where Martha and my close friends have made a big difference by giving me the strength and wisdom needed to maintain the integrity God demands.

When I think of the free enterprise system today—its broken character, integrity, and moral values—it's fun to imagine how much more efficient, productive, and profitable it could be if we had a great desire to run every organization with the kind of character and integrity God demands. If for no other reason, as good business people we should have the desire to run our companies that way. It just makes good long-term business sense.

We must remember as leaders in our chosen vocation that God's laws demand we take the gifts He has given us and hold them in great esteem and treat them with great value.

I often have to reflect in my own life these gifts are not mine; they were given to me by Him. My vocation was not my choice, but the one that God desired me to have. Doesn't it make sense that these gifts should be surrounded with the kind of integrity that will glorify Him?

God will also hold us responsible for the gifts He has given us. "To whom much is given, much will be required."

Perhaps most importantly, we must remember that the people He has placed around us have been chosen by Him and are our most precious responsibility. There will be a day when He asks us how we assumed the responsibilities He laid before us. I'm convinced that one of the greatest responsibilities of Christian free-enterprise leaders is to allow people with whom they do business to see the reflection of Jesus Christ in everything they say and do. Only when this is accomplished can we say with pride, "My balance sheet is His!"

Chapter Three

REFLECTIONS FOR THOUGHT

1. Am I dealing with a specific issue today where my integrity is being challenged? What should my strategy be?

2. How can I help my business improve its character?

3. What would a code of ethics look like for my business?

4. Who are my accountability partners?

SCRIPTURE REFERENCES

Psalms 26:1-3
Proverbs 10:9
Proverbs 20:7

ANGER IN THE BOARD ROOM

N ot every one has the ability to see through Christ's eyes. We are sometimes blind to the possibility that God places people in our lives for a reason—even those we don't like and who don't like us. Also, isn't it funny that we usually relegate negative traits to "turkeys"—those people with whom we disagree—and leave the better, more positive attributes for ourselves?

How do we love those who don't love us?

There are a lot of reasons why "turkeys" go unloved. Many of them are egotists who lack any sensitivity whatsoever. They may be rude and crude, or maybe just lazy, cheap, and stingy. And the grand turkey of them all can have more than one of these repugnant traits.

The real truth is that when we are forced to deal with these people, we're often able to grow both professionally and personally. I've frequently been challenged to develop patience and tolerance as I waited on God to see me through some trying relationships.

However, we all have to remind ourselves that we are far from perfect and that even though we have a relationship with Jesus

Chapter Four

Christ, we still must sometimes struggle with our old nature—as did the Apostle Paul. Indeed, in Romans 7 there is a graphic account of Paul's inability to break the bonds of human nature, even though he knew he was a child of God. If Paul had problems dealing with his humanity, can we expect to be different?

Before turning your back on a God-given opportunity for improving relationships, there are several "do's" and "don'ts" to consider:

1. Don't avoid challenges. Challenge always leads to change, and change is the prerequisite to growth. In the workplace we do not have the option to walk away from difficult relationships—we have to deal with them, and this can be career threatening. Even worse, it can tend to make us compromise our Christian standards. However, I also believe these situations can be character builders, if pursued properly. God can use us right where we are, as perfect examples of those who are capable of dealing with difficult circumstances.

2. Do mend broken relationships. Nothing paralyzes a person quicker than pent-up anger. Many times organizations have been crippled by underlying outrage. The aftermath of such hostility always leads to broken relationships. Such explosive anger is often devastating and debilitating.

I remember once walking into an office and asking an associate what the person next to him did. He said, "I don't know. We had an argument two years ago and we haven't spoken since."

If two associates working side by side can't resolve personal differences, that's tragic as well as unproductive. Because anger makes us less effective in business, it certainly makes sense to discipline ourselves to deal with it.

That doesn't always mean that you have to build a beautiful friendship with someone you aren't crazy about, but I do believe God expects us to make an effort to understand and deal with difficult people. It's only then that we can make peace with ourselves and with God.

3. Do respect God's commandments. The most important reason for dealing with anger and broken relationships is that

> Nothing paralyzes a person quicker than pent-up anger.

God has commanded us to do so. He is very specific throughout the scriptures that we are to love those who don't love us as well as those who are difficult to love because of who they are.

In the Sermon on the Mount, Jesus addresses this issue of anger when He says,

You have heard that it was said to the people long ago, "Do not murder, and anyone who murders will be subject to judgment." But I tell you that anyone who is angry with his brother will be subject to judgment. Again, anyone who says to his brother, "Raca," is answerable to the Sanhedrin. But anyone who says, "You fool!" will be in danger of the fire of hell. Matthew 5:21-22

Clearly Jesus equates the inner attitude of anger with the outward act of murder. He continues in the following verses to command us to be reconciled to our brother or face severe consequences.

In Matthew 5:43-45 Christ states,

You have heard that it was said, "Love your neighbor and hate your enemy." But I tell you: Love your enemies and pray for those who persecute you, that you may be sons of your Father in heaven. He causes his sun to rise on the evil and the good, and sends rain on the righteous and the unrighteous.

Jesus concludes this portion of the sermon with four penetrating questions challenging the practice of loving only those it is easy to love.

I believe we see the power of Christ working in us when we extend our hearts to someone we find it difficult to care about. I admit this doesn't come easy. After all, we're only human, so we have to work a little harder, drawing on God's strength, to build relationships with difficult people.

RELATIONSHIP-BUILDING STRATEGIES

There are two distinctly different relationship problems that crop up frequently in business: those dealing with a superior or peers, and those relating to subordinates. Each requires a differ-

Chapter Four

ent strategy.

The person on top. How do we deal with hard-to-like bosses or peers? Unless they lack integrity or ask us to do something immoral, I believe we have the charge to stretch ourselves to work with these people.

We all have inherent differences when it comes to personality and personal work habits. It might take a bit of finesse on your part, but it is possible to compensate without compromising your values or integrity. In this way you can demonstrate your desire to build a better relationship. That alone can make a major statement about the impact of Christ in your life.

Perhaps you may have a good relationship with your boss but are very different with regard to personality, temperament, work style, and priorities. Because of these contrasts, the relationship could be fragile. You need to recognize the potential potholes and make sure you don't fall into one.

For example, my former boss was the owner of our business and an entrepreneur I learned to sincerely respect. He realized that I came out of a business that was much larger, more organized, and more structured than his. As a result, we went about managing our companies in very different ways.

With such dissimilar styles, we both strived hard for mutual understanding. We made sure major decisions were discussed fully and that the company's best interests were always held above our differences.

There were many occasions when I said to my boss that I felt that our greatest competitor might be our relationship. Because of this, we both devoted time and energy to making ours a mutually beneficial association.

Fractured relationships can drain away the vitality of a company. It's a waste of power that could much better be channeled into improving the business.

The jobs I've held over the past twenty-five years have provided me with beautiful occasions to demonstrate Christ's love, and each one has been a ministry opportunity.

Christ knew the human heart well. He realized that people responded best to love. I think we have a responsibility to demonstrate Christ's love to those who don't know Him. And, like Christ, we can set an example that people will follow.

However, I have to admit there are times when this is very hard to do. I've worked for people who didn't have my best interests at heart. Some wanted to put me in a position where my deficiencies would be highlighted and subjected to ridicule. It wasn't as much a personal affront as it was their particular management tendency to diminish others to allow themselves to look better. I felt helpless, because to fight back meant I could get fired, transferred, and/or further humiliated. If I tried to hide by crawling into a shell, I could get lost in the corporate jungle and never be heard from again. I have often gotten through troubled times like these using a combination of prayer, love, and patience. God brought closure to the situations by either removing me from the problem or removing the problem from me and allowing adversarial conditions to mellow.

On the other hand, if you find you have a relationship with your boss that you cannot tolerate, or that is impairing your walk with Christ, you should seriously ask whether the work you're doing is really God's plan for you. God demands as a priority that our relationship with Him never be compromised.

I knew an executive who felt so degraded by his boss that he wanted to quit years ago. When I asked him why he didn't, he told me that he "loved the job security." Money is no collateral for security. If you have money but little self-worth, you will never feel safe, no matter how many dollars you make.

This executive lacked the confidence in himself to quit. He didn't understand that God is the only real security he would ever have. When we're faced with a difficult relationship, it may be a true opportunity to choose a better life. It may be God's way of telling us we need to move on. God truly wants us to have the freedom to enjoy our work and be the people He has called us to be.

Reaching out to associates. There are times when associates may feel threatened by their boss. If you're in management, the challenge here is to reach out to that person and show acceptance. It's your responsibility to create an environment where subordinates feel like they are part of the team and can express different ideas without fearing ridicule or retribution.

Management must set the standards for integrity and demand excellence in job performance, but we can do this without having our associates fear we are about ready to lower the boom. Working with people who aren't particularly likable can be a special opportunity for growth. One of the real joys in my life as a Christian is to be able to do the unexpected. When people do things that don't warrant our love, that's when it's fun to love them anyway.

When a subordinate deserves the third degree, that's the time to show compassion. Jesus was the master of doing the unexpected. As Christians we can follow the Master—and take the spiritual step of replacing anger with love.

REPAIRING BROKEN RELATIONSHIPS

We, as Christians, have the responsibility to be the initiator and the reconciler. Our indwelling Holy Spirit can help us overcome human inertia and prompt us to pray and initiate action. If we take our role as reconcilers seriously, we will make significant changes in the marketplace.

I'm absolutely convinced the businesses that succeed in today's environment aren't necessarily the ones with all the geniuses, but those that are comprised of a team united for a common purpose and cause. The harmony and relationships within that team maximize the productivity and potential of that organization.

Just as it makes good business sense to have oneness in our business, it makes good sense from an eternal perspective, too. There are three key ways to prevent and mend broken relationships:

1. Prayer. Prayer is our number one resource. Praying for the people who trouble you most is the strongest medicine available.

> If we take our role as reconcilers seriously, we will make significant changes in the marketplace.

In past years I've met people whom I've disliked. I suppose I could justify the reasons—I probably could say it was their fault. But, in reality, it was my reaction to their words and actions that caused my problem in the first place. I chose to respond to their anger in a negative way when I could have chosen another, more loving response that would have diffused the situation.

The Matthew 5 passages discussed earlier in this chapter place the responsibility on our shoulders to pray, whether we are right or not, regardless of the circumstances. It's a hard lesson to learn—but a most valuable one if we want to improve our lives.

Several years ago I was having a rough time with a company vice president. We never agreed on anything and were coming at each other like two roosters in a pit. It wasn't pretty, and I know it was unpleasant for our associates.

A good friend suggested to me that I put his name on my prayer list and pray for him daily. At first the thought of praying for the man made me laugh. Yet I went ahead and did it anyway. Well, guess what? The more I prayed, the more difficult it became for me to argue with him. My anger began to subside, and I started to understand why he disliked me.

As I mellowed in my attitude toward him, he slowly became more open with me. We never became best friends, but many of our associates could see the difference. Where we had once polarized our fellow associates, making the whole organization less productive, we started to build a better relationship that not only strengthened the company but our personal association as well.

God's answer to prayer doesn't always work out this way, however. More than once I've prayed for people who simply don't respond. Recently I prayed for an individual every day until my anger dissipated and I could appreciate him for what he was. However, there were many things in his life that were causing him turmoil. Although I wasn't the real target, his anger at me never did subside. In fact, it grew stronger, and to this day he remains bitter toward me. Yet I can honestly say I have replaced my own resentment with understanding, and I feel good about

Chapter Four

my decision to do so.

That's really all Jesus was talking about when he said to love your enemies. He was saying that it is not for them alone that you might love, but for yourself, and for the love of God. Only then can you find true peace within your own heart.

2. Building up an adversary. Building up your adversary can be a powerful way to help mend a broken relationship. We spend much of our lives in combat and very little time building others up. When we look at what we're really doing to ourselves and others, we can begin to alter our reactions to those around us. Not only will you surprise yourself, but you'll probably shock a lot of people out of their socks when you respond affirmatively rather than negatively. You'll send a message that you are trying to get into neutral territory and build a relationship. The results can be amazing.

When I first became a company president, I ran head on into a problem with my new boss. As chief executive officer he had chosen someone else for my job, but the man he picked was

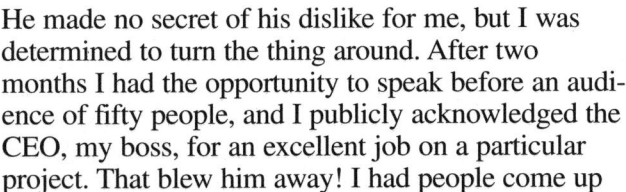

rejected, in turn, by his boss. The CEO didn't want me; that much I knew. And that was the start of an uneasy relationship between us.

He made no secret of his dislike for me, but I was determined to turn the thing around. After two months I had the opportunity to speak before an audience of fifty people, and I publicly acknowledged the CEO, my boss, for an excellent job on a particular project. That blew him away! I had people come up to me afterward who were convinced that we were totally reconciled. We never became great friends, but we were able to work together. I count that as a victory.

This strategy can be very helpful. But there is one very real obstacle to overcome: It's called pride. It takes maturity to look for opportunities to praise an adversary. But once pride is in the dust, you'll be surprised at how people respond to you.

3. Honesty with others and yourself. The third way to build a relationship is to be honest and straightforward with co-workers. Poor relationships often start with a misunderstanding.

There is always risk involved in sitting down with your opponent and talking things over, but I've personally found it a great way to overcome obstacles. Afterward, both of us usually feel a lot better.

Like cancer, broken relationships need to be treated. If you let the problem slide and pretend to ignore it, it won't go away. In fact, it's bound to get a lot worse. Scripture is very specific about dealing with this in that it tells us to make an attempt at reconciliation until God gives us another direction.

The definition of God's anger in Psalms 30:5 pretty much sums up the whole idea:

For His anger lasts only a moment, but his favor lasts a lifetime; weeping may remain for a night, but rejoicing comes in the morning.

There's no place for anger in the boardroom. God has voted it out, and so should we.

Like cancer, broken relationships need to be treated

Chapter Four

REFLECTIONS FOR THOUGHT

1. Do I have a relationship problem today? For whom can I pray? Whom do I need to build up?

2. Do I see a potential relationship problem on the horizon? What can I do to minimize the problem?

3. Do I see paralyzing anger in my company today? How is it affecting productivity? What can I do to change it?

4. How can I build better relationships with my family and friends?

SCRIPTURE REFERENCES

Romans chapter 7
Matthew 5:21-22
Matthew 5:43-45
Psalms 30:5

Chapter Five

CONDUCTING BUSINESS WITH THE OPPOSITE SEX

How do we interact with the opposite sex in the business environment?

The office was deserted. My secretary and most of our people had already left for the day. I was scrambling to get out the door to catch my train when I looked up to see one of my managers blocking the door. I'll never forget the look on his face. With bloodshot eyes and tie in disarray, he looked more dressed for a barroom skirmish than business in the executive suite.

I sat my briefcase down and asked him what his problem was. I knew I would be missing the next couple of trains when he replied, "I just need to talk for a few minutes."

Two hours later he finished his story. It wasn't pretty. What had begun over an innocent cup of coffee with his secretary had evolved into an intimate relationship that eventually destroyed a fifteen-year marriage, leaving three children at home without a father.

Most affairs usually start with such naivete. That man's first cup of coffee led into a conversation where personal aspects of each other's lives were shared, including the problems both of them were having with their spouses. Shortly after this, the two-

67

some began having occasional social dinners together. Next it was a date on the sly. Finally came the unplanned business trip and then the night at her apartment. Deceit led to more deceit, then tremendous guilt. After a year and a half it all came crashing down.

Their "wonderful relationship" had revolved around emotion, pity, and sex. Not only had they ruined their own lives, they had shattered a marriage and destroyed a family. There was no telling how many other people would be affected. Unfortunately, this story is not uncommon in today's work environment.

In talking with Christian men and women over the years, I've sensed a real openness to discuss issues like honesty, anger, and the danger of becoming workaholics. Yet there always seems to be some hesitation when it comes to bringing up struggles with immorality and lust. First, there seems to be a general reluctance to admit to the temptation; second, there seems to be an unwillingness to acknowledge that the marketplace, by its very nature, creates situations that make us more vulnerable to circumstances that may trap us in an unwanted relationship.

Most companies tend to shy away from any active involvement in preventing immorality on the job. In fact, the tendency is to look the other way and rarely provide safeguards to protect employees. It is therefore an individual's responsibility to be on guard.

When you analyze how the marketplace works, it's easy to see how improper relationships can develop and how, if we aren't careful, we can be swept away by our own unsuspecting desires. We need to be mindful of three fundamentals operating in most business environments:

1. Bonding. Most of us spend more hours each week with our associates than we do with our spouses. Many of the people with whom we work are of the opposite sex. Inevitably a bond develops that is necessary for success in the marketplace. Unfortunately, that same strength can become a real weakness if left unmanaged.

2. Emotion sharing. All of us spend a considerable amount of time with our associates in emotional turmoil. There are exhilarating highs pursuing opportunities and success. There are also the devastating lows when we lose an opportunity or fail. Often the people giving us the most encouragement are those with whom we work because they understand the problems and stress we face.

3. Goal sharing. People in the marketplace, by virtue of their position, are challenged to be intellectually sharp, to dress correctly, and to be aggressive. It is easy for those who work in the same environment to be comfortable and identify with them. Let's face it, it's exciting to be with people who share our goals and dreams in business. Again, what can be a key ingredient to achieving success in this environment can become a real personal stumbling block.

It's easy to convince ourselves that we are not vulnerable to intimate relationships. I really believe the minute you think you are not susceptible to desire, you are in trouble. All of us are capable of falling victim to our passion, given the right set of circumstances.

For example, I remember when one of my associates was getting ready to take a long business trip with an attractive department manager. This could have been the perfect setup for a potentially explosive situation. I took it upon myself to remind him of his responsibility. After returning from the trip, he thanked me for my concern.

Sexual harassment is another issue that can rear its ugly head. This was brought home to me during a recent plane trip when the attendant confided that she was having problems with the flight crew. Her job, she said, wasn't fun any more because she was often trapped in foreign cities with crew members whose intentions weren't exactly honorable.

She asked what our company's corporate policies were. I told her that our basic commitment is to protect our associates by making sure individuals in our company don't take advantage of our people. I told her we had proof that we backed our words with actions, because we have terminated some very productive associates due to the fact that they lacked the ethical character we demanded. I told her we had not taken this position because

> All of us are capable of falling victim to our passion, given the right set of circumstances.

the law required it, but rather because it was the right thing to do.

There are ways to limit our vulnerability, personally and in the corporate world. We each have personal choices to make that can protect us. There are three essential areas—spiritual health, individual action, and corporate action—that can help ensure that we do not get involved in immoral relationships.

SPIRITUAL HEALTH

Spiritual health is the most essential of any course of action. We need to establish and maintain our intimate relationship with God. We must start with trusting Christ as our personal Savior.

As we spend time getting to know God through Bible study and prayer, it will become more obvious to us when we are vulnerable. When we know this, we will have the knowledge we need to discipline our actions and protect ourselves.

When we recognize a situation that opens us up to temptation, we must seek God's help. Just repeatedly bringing our vulnerability before God in prayer will increase our awareness of the need to exercise caution in these matters.

I believe that we are more prone to making mistakes in our lives if we don't seek spiritual guidance. As we spend time getting to know God through Bible study and prayer, we develop a spiritual capacity that makes us less vulnerable to situations that can be harmful to us. When we bring our vulnerability before God in prayer and ask for His protection, we develop an intimacy with the Lord that is far greater than any relationship we might have with a co-worker.

We must realize God's great concern about the subject of lust. The New Testament writers urged the early church converts to avoid past lifestyles. They believed that leading a morally pure life would separate the believers from their pagan world. Both Peter and John dealt with the subject of moral purity and the impact a distinct lifestyle would have on the community.

In the book of Romans, Paul talks about the ability of Christians to resist evil desires because they have available the power of Christ. Paul urges believers to rely on the Lord Jesus Christ as the means to avoid the lusts of the flesh:

Rather, clothe yourselves with the Lord Jesus Christ, and do not think about how to gratify the desires of the sinful nature. Romans 13:14

The primary reason God is concerned about lust is what inevitably follows. The stages of sin are spelled out in James:

. . . but each one is tempted when, by his own evil desire, he is dragged away and enticed. Then, after desire has conceived, it gives birth to sin; and sin, when it is full-grown, gives birth to death. James 1:14-15

In other passages of Scripture this same scenario is played out. The sin of Adam and Eve in the garden, Achan in the Book of Joshua, and David with Bathsheba all began with evil desire that then led to sin. None of us can resist temptation alone. We aren't always strong enough to overcome our lustful impulses. So why take the chance?

INDIVIDUAL ACTION

Individually we must keep relationships with associates of the opposite sex on a business level. That sounds so basic, but it is an important point that many people miss. It sounds so innocent to have lunch. After all, you might say, "it's business." In my opinion, only on rare occasions should we be alone with an associate of the opposite sex in a social setting. Lunches, dinners, and/or cocktail parties that become "one-on-one" on a repeated basis can lead to trouble.

The things you talk about should be focused on the business of the day. When conversation strays from that, there's a tendency to become too personal. Knowledge that should be reserved for your spouse should not be shared with someone else.

Even idle conversation about dress or how an associate looks, if conducted beyond business needs, can become dangerous. When a business relationship becomes something more than what is necessary or appropriate, a problem can be just around

Chapter Five

the corner.

In addition, times will arise when it might be convenient to give an associate a ride home, a lift to the train or the airport, or transportation somewhere else. Again, it sounds so innocent. Once you get into the routine of being together without business reasons, your motives should be challenged.

When a business relationship becomes something more than what is necessary or appropriate, a problem can be just around the corner.

We should be aware that our greatest opportunities for failing are probably those times when our relationship with our spouse is not at its best. It is when we are feeling sorry for ourselves, a bit down and looking for sympathy, that we are most susceptible to immoral relationships. This becomes another great reason for trying always to improve our marriages. As I study Scripture and have a closer relationship with Christ, I continue to have a better appreciation for my responsibilities to my wife, Martha. Even when we may be having some disagreements or a difficult week, that spiritual perspective might be the encouragement I need to take the right path.

I'm not saying we should not be men and women of great compassion and understanding to those of the opposite sex. Certainly this is what God has called us to do. Yet Satan can take the noblest of causes and turn them into tragedy. We must look at ourselves as God's person in the marketplace and be careful to keep in check any kind of emotion that might develop into an unwanted predicament.

A few minutes of unbridled passion can lead to years of unhappiness. Lust can be so incredibly attractive, yet appearances are not all they're cracked up to be. What may look good on the surface can be very ugly underneath.

Some time ago a friend of mine confided that she had recently experienced a deep desire to do something that she knew she would regret later. However, she never acted upon the urge.

"What stopped you?" I asked her.

She thought for a long time, then said, "Jeff, it would have been an easy thing for me to do. But I knew it was wrong. Not only would it have eventually hurt the people I loved, but it would have hurt me as well. I knew down deep that having an affair, however brief, would really mix up my priorities and confuse me. I decided to pray about it and thankfully came to the conclusion that I was strong enough to say 'No.'"

Of course, our first responsibility is to Christ—then to our families and friends, including our associates. However, I sometimes think we forget we have an obligation to those to whom we may feel a strong attraction. It may look like a simple relationship or a real opportunity to share a joy that might be missing in our lives, but when left unchecked, this can provide Satan a tremendous opportunity to establish a destructive relationship, not a loving one. If a genuine affection develops, protect the other person by walking away from any opportunity to overstep the bounds of propriety. If we don't, the crash is inevitable.

CORPORATE ACTION

In the corporate environment, we can be limited in our influence, but we do not have to be invisible. If you are in a position of leadership in a company, take a position on immorality. If you don't have direct authority, encourage your company leaders to take a stand. Let it be known that you do not condone immoral behavior in the workplace. As godly men and women, we have an obligation to identify right and wrong. We must speak out for what is right.

Certain areas may be outside your control, but at least you will have taken a position and demonstrated character consistent with your Christian beliefs.

If you are in leadership, you can take personal responsibility for opposite-sex relationships in your company. Too many times business will give lip service to discouraging immoral relationships, but actions rarely follow the words. In fact, I think most companies would rather pretend immoral relationships do not exist than confront the offenders—especially where the guilty party is a "valued" executive.

Several years ago I heard rumors about a man who was married and reportedly having an affair with his secretary. In fact, it was becoming well known in the office. When confronted, he denied it. I had no choice but to accept his denial. As it turned out the rumors were true. Again I confronted him and told him it was going to have to stop. While I could not force him to change his personal life, I could alter his business relationship with his secretary.

This man had no idea how his actions had affected our associates' attitude toward him. He could not see that the position in which he had put himself made it impossible for him to succeed because of his immorality. When I confronted him with the issue, he became incensed and told me he would not end the relationship. I told him I would.

I'm sure he expected me to transfer his secretary. Instead, I terminated him for conducting himself in such a way that his department could not properly operate. Because of his conduct, an entire department of people had become less productive and were beginning to lose respect for the company. It was my responsibility to the company and our employees to take a stand against behavior detrimental to the entire organization.

I personally believe running a well-disciplined business with regard to sexual conduct not only leads to more productivity, but also adds a sense of character and integrity to the company. An undisciplined business puts people in an environment where they feel they can get away with less than acceptable standards, and decency suffers where there is a lack of accountability.

I am convinced that unchecked passions do more to cripple the productivity of businesses than the loss of any key executive. I have seen instances where good employees have become incapacitated or slowed down to the point of uselessness because of immorality. If for no other reason, our responsibility to shareholders and the company should encourage us to promote the highest moral standards. As Christians we have an additional obligation to identify sin for what it is and take a stand. The best reason to protect ourselves from immorality and lust is *Jesus said so!*

REFLECTIONS FOR THOUGHT

1. Can you think of a situation today in your place of employment where you could be vulnerable to the development of an unwanted relationship?

2. What should you do to protect yourself and the other person?

3. Do you see an associate who is vulnerable? How can you help?

4. What can you do today as a leader or an associate to take a stand on morality in your place of employment?

SCRIPTURE REFERENCES

Romans 13:14
James 1:14-15

Chapter Six

TAKING A RECESS FROM STRESS

By its very nature the free enterprise system is competitive and extremely dynamic. When you mix these two ingredients and stir vigorously, you usually come out with something called stress.

According to USA Today, work is the biggest source of stress in our lives. The article's survey of 501 adults conducted by Research & Forecasts, Inc. revealed that "36% say work is their main source of stress, followed by money (22%), children (10%), health (7%), marriage (5%), and parents (5%). Only 5% say they have no stress at all in their daily lives and 10% have a little." (I have to chuckle at that last 15 percent, who probably didn't tell the whole truth.)

We need to make sure when we enter the marketplace as God's missionaries that we understand we'll be dealing with some of the same stress that all individuals face. Only with that knowledge can we begin to equip ourselves for success in dealing with pressure.

One of the real tragedies today is that people really don't understand how and why stress is generated. More importantly,

How does stress affect us? How would God want us to deal with stress?

they don't understand how to deal with it. As their confusion grows they begin to react to the pressure of the marketplace. Understanding how stress builds and how to deal with it is key for our success in God's eyes.

It's important to understand where stress comes from in the free enterprise system, which by nature is competitive. This is where people invest money, time, and energy, and the system continually creates within itself an ever-changing dynamic environment.

EXTERNAL, INTERNAL, AND SELF-GENERATED STRESS

Stress can flourish easily either externally from competitors and investors or internally from superiors, peers, and subordinates. Pressure may also be self-generated, as we push ourselves continually to perform better.

External sources of stress (competitors and investors). Companies always push to produce the kind of earning ratios that will satisfy investors. This sets up an immediate kind of performance anxiety that eventually filters down to associates. This kind of pressure is not necessarily bad; in fact, it's what makes us strive to be better. However, when this competition begins to create an overly aggressive situation, it can lead to more stress for our associates and ourselves.

Internal sources of stress (superiors, peers, and subordinates). Competition does not just occur between companies, but also between associates as they vie for promotions and recognition. There is only one ladder to the top, and many will be trying to climb over the same rung at the same time.

In today's economic climate, with the recent increase of mergers and acquisitions and mid-level management retooling, there's no internal "surge protector" to stop the ever-escalating sense of urgency. Every day some large company announces cutbacks or operation scale-downs. As a result, more managers are being forced into early retirement or are being laid off. The few jobs on the way to the top are becoming even more sought after.

Self-generated stress. We generate our own pressure when we push ourselves to outperform everyone else for that promotion. We also fear losing our jobs if our performance doesn't meet with expectations. The constant worry we create from within can be our own worst enemy. It can cause anxiety, paranoia, depression—even panic attacks. Learning to manage stress takes time. It also takes some soul-searching. Not everyone has the same physical and mental temperament for the job. It takes all kinds to make our world what it is, and this diversity is what makes us, as individuals, so very special to God.

PROBLEMS IN THE FREE ENTERPRISE SYSTEM

By its very nature, the free enterprise system causes anxiety that often leads to stress. Add to this the potential of corrupt characteristics such as greed and irresponsibility and combine these with lack of purpose, a willingness to settle for less, and shallow, inverted thinking—and you have a destructive domino effect that eventually may lead to sin.

Epidemic of greed. The proliferation of greed and selfishness is depleting our energy and dissipating principles that once taught us to work hard today so we can build our dreams tomorrow.

Our soaring national debt is a fitting symbol of our inability to curb the desire to have it all—immediately and without consequence. Likewise in recent years, national debt, consumer debt, and business debt has ruined many enterprises and plunged both businesses and individuals into bankruptcy.

Lack of responsibility. In America's early days, the vast majority of entrepreneurs and corporate leaders felt a real sense of responsibility to their businesses, consumers, investors, and employees. Today that accountability is often missing. Many business leaders no longer feel that they should be answerable for their actions.

Lack of purpose. Often there is a real lack of purpose that permeates our free enterprise system. Initially companies had a purpose for being, and this is why the free enterprise system was successful. These companies supplied work along with a reasonable return for their investors, and they produced a product with a purpose. The intangible quality that went hand in hand with

It takes all kinds to make our world what it is, and this diversity is what makes us, as individuals, so special to God.

purpose was a sense of pride in one's work, one's company, and one's product.

Today the free enterprise system seems to be at odds with its purpose. Sometimes business transactions seem to have no objective at all with regard to employees, investors, the company, or the product itself.

Willingness to settle for less. Many people are no longer willing to go that extra mile to produce a quality product or satisfy the customer. Some businesses don't look at discipline as a virtue, but rather as an inconvenient hindrance that might cause the bottom line to suffer.

Shallow, inverted thinking. Instead of holding fast to the helm of principle and discipline, many companies today are succumbing to competitive pressures. They are increasingly preoccupied with profit, thinking only of the present instead of looking ahead at the long-term health of business and the economy. Many organizations no longer care how their actions affect their people, their businesses, or the free enterprise system.

The world is all too eager to close in on us and we need to take a step back and really look at what is happening. Only then can we see how today's market can pressure us into making mistakes. One way to avoid the pitfalls of pressure is to be mindful of God's goals.

GOAL-SETTING UNDER PRESSURE

Negative thinking always makes a demanding situation more difficult and escalates the potential for problems. A major solution is to stay positive with an abundance of prayer. As Christians, shouldn't we put ourselves in a position to deal with stress in a more Christ-like way? I believe we should have two goals in dealing with pressure and stress:

1. To be the men and women God has called us to be.
2. To allow our actions to reflect God's grace.

All of us have had times of stress in our lives. I remember when I was the new chief financial officer for a retail division of a large conglomerate. At one particular meeting each of the CFOs was to make a presentation on improving productivity in a major accounting area.

My subject was accounts payable—something that doesn't exactly elicit passion in many people. Here I was in the company of men who had more experience in accounting and in making presentations than I ever imagined and I was supposed to take center stage with them as my audience.

As I witnessed the first three presentations that morning, the speakers impressed me with their content and poise. I began to feel ill-equipped. Fear crept in, followed by all-out panic.

My presentation was to be the first after lunch, so I skipped the meal (since it would have been be impossible to keep food down) but I didn't skip prayer. In fact, I prayed a lot that day.

When it was time for my presentation, I was barely able to talk. My controller asked, "Are you OK, Jeff? You look like you're ready to faint."

As I walked to the podium I remember saying to myself, "This is it. I'm about to wipe out, and I'll never live this down. Lord help me."

I opened with a feeble joke, but when the snickers began to fade I felt as if someone grabbed me, stood me up straight, and pushed me to the front of the platform. I was startled to hear myself say, "You guys may think you know accounts payable, but today I'm going to make you all experts."

Thirty minutes later I walked off the platform to hearty applause, the equivalent of a standing ovation for accountants. When I sat down my controller complimented me on a fantastic job.

"How did you do that?" he asked, rather astonished.

I looked at him and with a grin of confidence replied, "I didn't."

Chapter Six

OPPORTUNITIES FOR TAKING A RECESS FROM STRESS

As stated, the free enterprise system is competitive and relentless. As Christians we can either allow it to chew us up and spit us out, or we can take it for what it is and master it with the great principles He has given us in His word.

My eight opportunities for relieving or avoiding stress certainly are not all-inclusive, but I have found they offer a better understanding what kind of decisions He wants us to make.

When I reflect on these principles, God allows me to have a tremendous peace—and a sense of His presence and grace. Frequently it's been that peace which has given me the perseverance to stand in the gap for Him and to reflect His desires in a world of unresolve.

That being said, let me share these opportunities with you:

1. My Opportunity for a Best Effort

Let the word of Christ dwell in you richly as you teach and admonish one another with all wisdom, and as you sing psalms, hymns and spiritual songs with gratitude in your hearts to God. And whatever you do, whether in word or deed, do it all in the name of the Lord Jesus, giving thanks to God the Father through him. Colossians 3:16-17

Being under pressure brings out the best in most people. It challenges us and puts us on the cutting edge, harnessing our talents and honing our insight. This driving force can be an opportunity to maximize our resources and allow us to accomplish even more than we envisioned or ever thought possible. When the going gets tough, we want to be able to look back and say—win, lose, or draw—"I gave it my all."

Every one of us can review our lives and see where we went through some deep water: job difficulties, family crises, or personal setbacks. These were all great opportunities to reach inside and pull a little harder. It's encouraging to look back and know we were able to weather some pretty good storms and give our best effort in the process.

A great way to remember some of these milestones or significant times in our lives is to do what God's chosen people, the Israelites, did in the Old Testament. When a crisis had passed, they named the location with a descriptive title or left a monument as a tangible reminder of the event. These tangible reminders of historic incidents had a major impact on their lives and the lives of their followers.

When Abraham was spared from sacrificing Isaac, he named the place where he had constructed the altar "The Lord Will Provide." This was a permanent reminder of God's faithful provision.

After Joshua led the children of Israel into the promised land, a monument of twelve stones was left as a sign to those who followed of God's faithfulness to His people.

I have my own modern-day version of this kind of story. When the John Wanamaker Company merged with another firm, I, as the president, had the unfortunate job of liquidating hundreds of jobs prior to my own departure. In the midst of this, what I would define as the two most stressful years of my career, I found two opportunities: the first was being able to minister to hundreds of associates I respected and loved, and the second was a chance to trust Christ.

Today in our home library is a bronze eagle statue, the symbol of John Wanamaker's that reminds me of the two years when I was called to stand in the gap for those I cared for. We all need to have some way to remember those tough times when God provided extra strength or courage just to see us through situations when He enabled us to accomplish things that would have been impossible without His support.

Some of my greatest satisfactions in past years were not necessarily dependent on winning the game; rather, they came when I put forth my best effort, knowing it was the best I could do. That is what God requires from us. We need to keep on trucking even when the chips are down. We need to honor Him with our best effort.

> We need to keep on trucking even when the chips are down. We need to honor Him with our best effort.

Chapter Six

2. My Opportunity to Shine

You are the light of the world. A city on a hill cannot be hidden. Neither do people light a lamp and put it under a bowl. Instead they put it on its stand, and it gives light to everyone in the house. In the same way, let your light shine before men, that they may see your good deeds and praise your Father in heaven.
Matthew 5:14-16

Our greatest testimony does not necessarily come from our speeches, our thoughts, or our ministries; rather it comes from our actions. When we're under pressure, we are being keenly watched by our associates who are aware of our motives and are especially interested in how we react to difficult situations.

Several years ago the company for whom I worked was under the gun by the board to improve earnings. I felt what the board wanted from us was impossible. That year, as I prepared my presentation for them, the thought entered my mind that I could embellish our programs, making our strategies look better than they were. That would have alleviated the pressure on me. As I prepared my talk my secretary informed me that several executives were curious to know how honest I would be with the board.

Instead of elaborating on the programs, I thought I would honestly tell the board what I felt we could accomplish in the coming year. What a beautiful opportunity to shine! I was glad that my associates were there to keep me honest. A week before the board meeting I gave my presentation to twenty key executives and asked them to challenge any strategy they believed was more of a stretch than we could accomplish.

One executive remarked that our strategies were going to be difficult, but he was willing to give it a go if I was. Another thanked me for being honest with them and the board.

If we are serious about our testimony, pressure and stress may often give us an opportunity to be the light and shine for the world to see.

3. My Opportunity to Demonstrate Integrity

The law of the Lord is perfect, reviving the soul.
The statutes of the Lord are trustworthy, making wise the simple.
The precepts of the Lord are right, giving joy to the heart.
The commands of the Lord are radiant, giving light to the eyes.
The fear of the Lord is pure, enduring forever.
The ordinances of the Lord are sure and altogether righteous.
They are more precious than gold, than much pure gold; they
are sweeter than honey, than honey from the comb.
By them is your servant warned; in keeping them there is great
reward. Psalms 19:7-11

As Christians we have an opportunity to demonstrate integrity. We cannot afford to compromise our character, no matter what the competition. During times of intense pressure, we are vulnerable, and that's when we may be tempted to do things we know we shouldn't. Yet, this also can be our opportunity to really stand up for Christ. Not only to excel at our jobs, but to excel at exhibiting a proper set of moral standards.

It's tempting, of course, to take the immoral route, to build case after case for taking the wrong road. It usually begins subtly, but with enough thought, energy, and Satan's help, we can always justify the means. Yet no matter how far along the wrong path we go, we need to always remember that God allows U-turns.

Stress can break us down. It can fatigue us. During stressful times in my own life, I've found that only the grace of God has allowed me to do that which pleases Him.

We must also remember that intense situations produce great opportunities for defeating Satan—a fight our associates may be closely watching. As the old saying goes, actions do speak louder than words.

4. My Opportunity to Build Character

Consider it pure joy, my brothers, whenever you face trials of
many kinds, because you know that the testing of your faith

Chapter Six

develops perseverance. James 1:2-3

There are times in one's life where God really builds character. Sometimes pressure and competition are the things God places before us to allow us to become who He wants us to be. I often think if life wasn't full of little potholes, we might not find the inner strength to be closer to God. From that perspective alone we should all be able to sense a peace in our trials.

I have a friend who recently had to file for personal bankruptcy. His family relationships became frayed, his business opportunities were significantly reduced, and his life was turned upside down.

As he struggled through the mire, he endured a lot of deep emotional pain and embarrassment. His pride was stripped away. Yet today he is a new man, more committed to Christ than ever. He speaks about how his experience changed his character, goals, and motives in life. He is the first to say that he never wanted his painful ordeal, but in fact, it was this very experience that made him take a hard look at his priorities.

None of us want to ask for that kind of experience, but sometimes that is exactly the kind of drastic action God needs to take to get our attention. Fortunately, He loves us enough to do whatever is necessary to bring us back to Him.

I often say when we leave this world we should only be remembered by two things: our relationship with Christ, and our character.

5. My Opportunity to Trust My Spouse and Friends

Let us hold unswervingly to the hope we profess, for he who promised is faithful. And let us consider how we may spur one another on toward love and good deeds. Let us not give up meeting together, as some are in the habit of doing, but let us encourage one another—and all the more as you see the Day approaching. Hebrews 10:23-25

When I am dealing with a problem that needs wise counsel, I find this is a great opportunity to use the close network of people who really care about me.

> When we leave this world we should only be remembered for two things: our relationship with Christ, and our character.

Martha, my wife, has been a great resource over the years and probably the most important person in my life who listens and cares about me. If we truly believe marriage is a partnership, we need to learn to cultivate special relationships with our spouses. After all, they are the ones who live with us and share our goals and dreams.

I also mentioned elsewhere in this book that I have a couple of good friends who know me well. No matter how difficult the situation, they are always willing to listen. Many times the counsel received from these good friends has made the difference in whether I succeed or fail.

Covenant relationships are important in today's fast-moving world. These deep and important friendships can be life-savers. The Bible mentions several of these relationships. In the Old Testament, David had Jonathan. In the New Testament, Paul had Timothy. Even Jesus had a special friendship with three of the Apostles. In each of these examples the relationship exceeded friendship and extended to putting one's life on the line for the other.

How many people do you know who would risk their life for you? Who would you risk your life for? When I look back over my life, I am grateful for Martha and the men God has brought to guide me during the difficult times.

We cannot maximize our potential without covenant friends. If you have one, praise God. If you don't, ask that He might give you one!

We shouldn't be limiting God's desire to love us.

6. My Opportunity to Kneel in Prayer

Cast your cares on the Lord and he will sustain you; he will never let the righteous fall. Psalms 55:22

Whenever we are under great strain, we need to remember our greatest asset is prayer. God expects us to use our resources, maximize our best efforts, and be obedient—but He also expects us to pray.

When Nehemiah went before King Artaxerxes distressed about the condition of his people and his home, he had already prayed about the opportunity to bring his request to the king. Yet when the king asked him what he wanted, Nehemiah immediately prayed before answering. He got what he wanted and the rest is history. The point is that Nehemiah put prayer first and action second.

I love the comfort, courage, and conviction prayer can bring to my life when stress is trying to own it. Prayer allows me to again put life into perspective. Does it release us from all pain and anxiety? Of course not. But it does help take the situation and put it into proper focus.

Prayer also allows our Father to talk with us. We are still His children, and as adult as we might feel, we still need our Father, much more than our children need us. We shouldn't be limiting God's desire to love us.

Of course Jesus was our greatest role model. In Luke 5:16 we get a glimpse of the importance of prayer to our Lord. After healing hundreds of people and feeling the burdens of the multitudes, Jesus had to get away. Unlike us He did not get away just to vacation. As the verse says, *but He Himself would often slip away to the wilderness and pray.* Even the Son of God needed to be alone with his Father.

There is a saying that I love to use: *Work on it as if it all depended on me. Pray on it as if it all depended on Him.* Prayer, prayer, prayer—what a powerful source to sustain us in our time of need!

7. My Opportunity to Trust His Plan

Trust in the Lord with all your heart and lean not on your own understanding; in all your ways acknowledge him, and he will make your paths straight. Proverbs 3:5-6

When we are in difficult situations, we need to remember that God knows where we are. Sometimes we feel so trapped it seems like the walls are coming down and nobody cares. We want to somehow shift the blame, so we cry out, "God, why did you put me here?"

We cannot blame God, however, when we encounter pressure. It's important to accept that we don't always have control over the failure of a company or the loss of a loved one. God doesn't necessarily cause things to happen, but He does allow them to happen. Yet throughout those troubled times, even as painful as they are, we can always remember that He loves us, and we still need to trust in Him.

A challenge that may seem negative at first may turn out to be very positive. I was living in Miami when I got a phone call from a company with a division in Philadelphia. They needed a chief financial officer. I didn't want to move to Philadelphia—I liked Miami. A week later they called back and said they really wanted to meet me and talk about the job. I told them I would fly out, but I wasn't really interested in moving.

It wasn't until much later I discovered that the man scheduled to interview me and be my superior in Philadelphia wasn't too excited about me coming as a candidate for the job since I lacked the experience he thought necessary for the position. But for some reason, which neither of us understood at the time, he reluctantly agreed to interview me.

The interview went well and we had an enjoyable conversation. Then my interviewer asked what Martha did. I told him she was on staff for "Young Life," a Christian youth organization, and his whole perspective changed.

We launched into a lengthy discussion about our faith. Suddenly my lack of experience didn't matter quite as much. And just as suddenly I thought Philadelphia might not be such a bad place after all.

I had never worked for a man who put his faith into practice and displayed values the way this man did. When I left Philadelphia that night he said to me, "In all my years in retail, I don't think I've ever told anyone this on the first interview, but I want you to go to work for me."

I explained to him that at first I felt I didn't want anything to do with Philadelphia, but that the place was starting to grow on me.

When I walked into our home back in Miami, Martha said,

> God doesn't necessarily cause things to happen, but He does allow them to happen.

Chapter Six

"You don't even have to tell me. We're going to Philadelphia!"

Literally in a matter of days we sold our house in Miami and bought another one in the City of Brotherly Love. At each step I felt God telling me that he wanted me in this new place and that He was going to open every door along the way.

As it turned out our nine years in Philadelphia became one of the most gratifying times in our lives. God allowed some significant challenges along with some great opportunities, but most importantly, He allowed us to depend on Him.

8. My Opportunity to Acknowledge His Sovereignty

For I know the plans I have for you, says the Lord. They are plans for good and not for evil, to give you a future and a hope. In those days when you pray, I will listen. You will find me when you seek me, if you look for me in earnest. Jeremiah 29:11-13 *(Living Bible)*

Sometimes when we are under pressure, it presents our greatest opportunity to acknowledge God as our Lord and Savior. When we begin to appreciate the fragility of life, its fleeting nature and sometimes desperate situations, we can take comfort in His sovereignty and look forward to the eternity He promises.

He knows where we are and He knows what we need. More importantly, He knows the kind of person He wants us to be. He knows exactly what He wants us to accomplish. He will provide just the right amount of resources at just the right time to accomplish His sovereign plan.

I think the Apostle Peter gave us the ideal perspective for Christian living on this planet. In his first letter to the early church, Peter identifies his readers as aliens and strangers. In other words, they were not citizens of this world, but their true residence was elsewhere. He was saying that our real home is in heaven and that we're here visiting for a short time as His messengers.

Today we issue "green" cards to those who have permission to be in this country temporarily. Our foreign residents live by our laws and have certain responsibilities, but they are not U.S.

citizens. As Christians we have a "green" card for this world. We are here temporarily for a specific purpose, but ultimately we will go home to heaven.

Peter doesn't leave us without some encouragement. In the first chapter of his letter he states our new birth through Christ guarantees us two things: first, a living hope, a firm conviction that we will spend eternity with Christ; second, an inheritance that is permanent. Our future is secured by the power of God, for His sovereignty assures us the future is as He described in His Word.

God's plans for us are set, and they are good. Our responsibility is to pray and seek out God in sincerity. If you really believe, then no circumstance or difficulty should shake your resolve to live for Christ.

My own determination to begin to live the kind of life God wanted for me began ten years ago on a cold, lonely night in a New York hotel room. It was the middle of January. I had to attend a business conference and I didn't want to be there. I'd just lost my job as president of John Wanamaker's and I was feeling embarrassed and depressed. For two days, I had to field the same question from a hundred different people who asked me what I was going to do now that I'd been let go. Every time they asked me that question, I felt like someone was stabbing me with a knife. I wasn't bleeding: I was hemorrhaging.

That night I was supposed to go out to dinner and I just couldn't do it. I sat on the edge of my bed and I wept for a long time. When I finished, I got up and walked over to the window. Snow was blowing everywhere and I could see the prostitutes plying their wares on the street corner. It's so hard when you're hurting and all alone. Finally, I sat down at a little desk and I took my Bible out and started flipping through it. I began to write some things down on a notepad. After a while I looked at my watch and saw that it was 2:00 a.m. I had been reading the Bible for over three hours! I'd never done that in my entire life. And what I scratched down on that piece of paper were these eight opportunities that you've just read. God had taken me into the Bible and given me these scriptures. Afterward I felt I heard Him say to me, "Jeff, it's OK. You can go to sleep now."

> If you really believe, then no circumstance or difficulty should shake your resolve to live for Christ.

Chapter Six

Thirty days later I met a wonderful gentleman from the Midwest. He had a seventy-year-old jewelry business and said he needed some help. It looked like a good fit. Today Helzberg Diamonds is the most productive jewelry business in America, with 165 stores nationwide. Recently it became a subsidiary of one of the country's most blue chip companies, Berkshire Hathaway.

God had a plan for my life. I don't know what His plan is for yours, but be open to looking at what it may be. No matter how difficult things may seem, God will see you through, if you let him lead the way.

Remember that these eight opportunities are not all-inclusive: you may have eight more of your own! Realize that God doesn't want our world to close us down. He has given us the wisdom to understand that stress is real, and he has provided us with the resources to prevail. Our Father truly does love us as His children.

As Paul says in Romans 8:37, *"in all these things we are more than conquerors through Him who loved us."*

REFLECTIONS FOR THOUGHT

1. Do I feel stressed out today? What is causing it?

2. Can I remember over the past six months situations where I felt great pressure? What was the cause?

3. Can I see areas in my own life where these opportunities to overcome stress could have been exercised? How might they have helped?

4. How might I have altered my life through these opportunities?

5. What are some specific things I can do to relieve tension in my life today?

SCRIPTURE REFERENCES

Colossians 3:16-17
Matthew 5:14-16
Psalms 19:7-11
James 1:2-3
Hebrews 10:23-25
Psalms 55:22
Luke 5:16
Proverbs 3:5-6
Jeremiah 29:11-13
Romans 8:37

FINDING GOD'S SOVEREIGN PLAN FOR OUR LIVES

Another church mission conference was over and I felt guilty. We had spent the whole week talking about the desperate need for missionaries in the Third World—about sending people to Africa, Asia, and Latin America. I couldn't relate to the discussion. I felt like I was trying to put a puzzle together and didn't have all the pieces. I struggled, knowing the closest I would ever come to being a real life missionary was through prayer and giving financially.

After several weeks of wrestling with this subject, I woke up one night and thought, hey, wait a minute! Why am I feeling guilty? I *am* a missionary. I don't have to go to Africa or any other country. I work every day in a mission field, right here in the marketplace. I'm convinced God has called me to be here just the same as He calls others to foreign lands.

I thank God for all His missionaries and support them financially and through prayers.

But nothing lessens our responsibility to be God's person in the marketplace. If we believe God has called us to be here, we need to understand He has a plan for our lives.

How do we find His sovereign plan? The unbeatable trinity: prayer, God's Word, and fellowship.

Chapter Seven

It is not enough just to draw closer to the Lord—we must glorify Christ in everything we do. We are His representatives on the sales force, as secretaries, as senior officers, or in whatever our positions might be.

How do I find the plan that God has for me? And once I discover it, how do I stay on course? There are as many ways for God to reveal His plan as there are people. He doesn't always work the same way, but several constants exist in every Christian's life. The setup is similar to baseball in that three outfielders are required, with each player having a distinct yet similar purpose.

My center fielder is prayer, which includes an intimate relationship with God that allows me to live life the way He would want me to live it.

My left fielder is the Bible. With God's Word, I can more easily distinguish between what He wants me to do and what the world wants me to do.

The right fielder, like the left fielder, is also important. Here I would put my covenant relationships, which encourage me, instruct me, and hold me accountable.

In order to play well, we need all three of these components for a successful game.

PRAYER

Prayer opens the door to a successful walk with the Lord. As in baseball, where a good center fielder provides the thread that solidifies the entire outfield, prayer can saturate our lives and overcome many shortcomings. Paul says,

Do not be anxious about anything, but in everything, by prayer and petition, with thanksgiving, present your requests to God. And the peace of God, which transcends all understanding, will guard your hearts and your minds in Christ Jesus. Philippians 4:6-7

I love the last part about keeping constant guard of our hearts and minds as they rest in Jesus Christ. Prayer is of the utmost importance to us, yet so many Christians lack a real intimate prayer life with Jesus Christ.

He may be our Savior and we may worship Him, but there can be no intimacy with God if our lives are not girded by prayer.

In the first fifteen years of my Christianity, I kept Christ at arm's length. I knew He was the sovereign God, but I didn't have an intimate and close relationship with Him. That was a tragedy. I am now beginning to understand He wants to have a close relationship with each of us. He wants to be our closest friend—one who loves us unconditionally.

He will understand when others don't. He will encourage us when no one else is there.

He will hold us accountable to be the righteous people He desires us to be.

There is no other way to achieve that intimate relationship without prayer. Prayer is the absolute cornerstone. Through both success and failure, I've learned some significant things about prayer in my own life:

1. We must find quality time to be with the Lord alone. I was one of those guys who prayed on the move as the car headed down the freeway. God told me one day that this was dangerous and a waste of my time—and maybe His. It finally dawned on me that I needed time to be with God when I was sharp and alert—time without interruption so my thoughts would be clear. For me that means waking up at 5:30 instead of 6:15 to have quality time with the Lord.

Most great relationships we have with people result from spending quality time with them. The same thing should be true of our relationship with Jesus Christ. We need to spend time developing a great relationship with Him.

2. We don't need to be constantly talking. My greatest revelations have come when I stopped talking and started listening to God. I have to remind myself of the day I felt Him say to me, "Jeff, would you please stop babbling. If you will give me a

> He will understand when others don't. He will encourage us when no one else is there.

chance to get a word in edgewise, you might understand what I want you to do." It's amazing sometimes how much God can teach us when we're just plain quiet.

That was a great lesson for me. One of the things that can come about from listening to God is a tremendous peace that sets the tone for your whole day.

3. Our prayers need to be more praise and less petition. In the past my prayers resembled a bad ball score: Petitions, 90; Praise, 10.

After I started reading the Scripture, I realized who God really was and I began to acknowledge Him more and more in my prayers.

Now more than half of my time with the Lord is spent praising Him and thinking about what I do have, rather than what I don't have. Remember, we can be comforted in knowing His awareness of the burdens of our heart. I really believe God has asked us to be faithful and spend quality time praising Him and rejoicing in the salvation He has given us.

A good exercise to help change the focus of our prayer life is to read through the Psalms and see how much time the psalmist spent praising God and offering thanksgiving. We can pray those same prayers every day.

4. Prayer must be a significant part of our life. I really believe prayer increases in meaning as it becomes significant in our lives. Once it becomes the mainstay of your life, you may find it necessary to give up those things that are really unimportant.

Prayer is the primary instrument in developing an intimate relationship with Jesus Christ.

If I am committed to my priorities of faith, family, friends, and vocation, I need to understand and recognize my prayer time is a nonnegotiable item. The minutes or hours I spend in dialogue with Jesus Christ is so vital to me, other schedules and events might have to be sacrificed or rescheduled.

5. We need to have an attitude of prayer all day. It is frightening to think how many major business, personal, and community decisions we make without ever going to the Lord for direction, wisdom, or knowledge. I try to take a few seconds and talk to my Heavenly Father as the need arises.

The Apostle Paul speaks clearly of continually being in prayer and urges believers to do the same. It's important for me to spend at least thirty to forty-five minutes with the Lord every morning. Yet, it isn't the quantity of time you spend with God that is so important; it's the quality of that time that matters.

I also find that one of the most effective uses of prayer for me is the spontaneous prayer.

In the Old Testament, Nehemiah gives a terrific example of a man constantly communicating with God through short but specific prayers. In an exchange with the King of Persia, Nehemiah provides us with the first "arrow" or spontaneous prayer as he quickly and silently prays before answering the king's question. That is the kind of prayer attitude we all need. These silent prayers usually consist of only a few words or sentences, but they are lifesavers. I have been in situations where I needed wisdom, some help to overcome confusion, and I just lifted up that need in brief, quiet prayer.

Nothing, I think, pleases God more than knowing we depend on Him. As you develop your relationship with Him through prayer, I believe you will see He honors those little intervals we spend with Him during the day.

6. We need to develop our own personal prayer book. Prayer is too important a topic to leave to chance with a "hit-or-miss" approach. It is essential to keep some form of written record of prayers and answers.

Years ago a good friend encouraged me to write down my primary praises and petitions each month, so I started a loose-leaf notebook. The first month's sheet had eight entries. Now I use both sides of a page for each month, and divide it up into "Praise or Thanks," "Repentance," "Personal Petitions," and "Intercessory Petitions."

Chapter Seven

This simple concept provides a beautiful method of organizing your thoughts and enables you to pray systematically. Even more important, this provides a written record of how God has answered your prayers. Today it would be difficult for me to live without my prayer book.

Hardly a day goes by without it getting my attention. Included in the Appendix (page 146) is an example of my personal prayer book.

When you are committed to prayer, you can begin to establish a real intimate relationship with God, which allows Him to reveal His sovereign plan for you. It might be a decision right in front of you or it might be a vision for the future. To help begin the process, remember that the six points we just mentioned above serve one purpose—to help us develop a consistent, quality prayer time. I have found the importance of building the intimate relationship with Jesus Christ can only come through prayer. Without that center fielder, we're never going to know what God might want us to do today or in the years ahead.

Building a new life based on prayer takes time and discipline.

A short word of encouragement for those who have not yet started a prayer journey. Let me encourage you to start slowly and avoid disappointment. No one hits a home run the first time up.

In baseball, the process begins with a bat and a ball and an understanding of the position you play. Over time you establish a batting average, and a home run becomes a possibility. However, when we hear how someone else prays or spends time in Bible study, we often try to adopt their patterns for our life. Each of us is unique to God, though, and thus we must move on our own path and chart our own course, at our own pace, in our own time, and do the best we can.

Building a new life based on prayer takes time and discipline. A goal of consistent, quality prayer time can easily be established. Don't force yourself to pray a certain amount of time the first day. Start with a few minutes, and then build by five or ten minutes every week or so until you reach the goal you have set. You'll be surprised how easily the time will increase. If you miss a day occasionally, don't be discouraged. Be encouraged by the days you have spent time with the Lord. He will honor your efforts as you follow the six points just described.

GOD'S WORD

My left fielder is the Word of God, the Bible. In our baseball analogy, the left fielder joins the center fielder in forming the nucleus of a successful defensive outfield. Good teams must have a dependable left fielder, one who can make a lot of plays in support of the center fielder. God's Word certainly supports an active prayer life in bringing us closer to Christ.

The Apostle Paul captured the essential nature of Scripture in his second letter to his disciple Timothy:

All Scripture is God-breathed and is useful for teaching, rebuking, correcting and training in righteousness, so that the man of God may be thoroughly equipped for every good work. 2 Timothy 3:16-17

I have the firm conviction that if we are going to be able to grasp what God wants us to do with our lives, we have to know the Bible. Learning the faith and helping us avoid heresy requires the Bible. Keeping us on the right course and learning to live in ways that are pleasing to God demands the Bible. Again, Paul clearly stated the need for Scripture to equip us to live for God. His Word is a blueprint for us. It is our personal spiritual plan.

For many years my idea of Bible study was to read a few verses every day or so or to attend an organized study session. Normally I had the opportunity to hear the Word on Sunday morning. I never truly felt the Bible had anything to do with me personally—certainly not as a plan for my life!

For some reason, it never occurred to me what God wanted to tell me about my personal life and what He wanted me to avoid. How he really wanted me to live was between the covers of His Book, where I could find His carefully written plan specifically designed for me.

If someone came to my office with a detailed business plan,

asking me to invest $10,000 in the venture, I guarantee you I would read the plan from cover to cover, probably more than once. I would have all kinds of questions to ask. Before investing my money, I would have all my questions answered. I would need to feel certain that I was going to get a good return on my dollars.

Isn't the investment of our lives more significant than money? Aren't we concerned about getting the best return on what we have claimed for ourselves? Why do we spend so little time searching for a direction that can bring joy and fulfillment to our lives?

I know the answers to the first two questions. I struggle to understand the reasons for the third. I have, however, come to appreciate my own need to get serious about understanding God's Word and then following the directions He gives me. In my own search, I've found four important things that have made a significant impact in my life:

1. I need to spend time reading the Bible every day.
Personally, I like to take about 15 minutes of my prayer time reading God's Word. There are several methods I've found helpful in giving me discipline. One is to read through the Bible beginning with Genesis. Another is to rotate between the Old and New Testaments, devoting several days to each individual section. Another is to find a book or study guide through a regular reading program. The important thing is to *get started.*

Don't put pressure on yourself to do more than you're able. Build your study habits slowly, over a period of time that feels right to you.

Read with pen in hand, underline key scriptures, and write your thoughts down in the margin. Treat your time in the Bible as if God were sitting beside you talking to you. I ask Him to illuminate my mind and help me understand His insights about dealing with my family.

I also ask how to overcome temptation in my life, or how to conduct myself in a difficult business transaction.

If you are serious about finding God's sovereign plan for your life and for developing a vision of how God could use you, then I honestly believe spending time each day with His Word is integral to one's peace of mind.

2. I need to have a system for digging a little deeper into God's Word. A concentrated study of a particular book or passage of Scripture is needed to thoroughly understand what God is saying. Studying with a group, your spouse, or close friends always helps. This gives you a chance to exchange thoughts and ask questions. We should take time to read commentaries and explore Bible dictionaries with a desire to gain a comprehensive understanding of the Scripture.

3. I need to memorize Scripture. Instant recall of an important piece of Scripture in times of need can be helpful. Memorizing Scripture may seem tedious at first, but in the long run it can be a lifesaver. God has brought me through some real crises in the past few years, and certain passages of Scripture have been helpful in carrying me past the painful times.

Now I'm able to share my discoveries with friends who are crossing some of the same deserts God brought me across. Memorizing those special verses remind me of God's faithfulness and His comfort and wisdom in difficult circumstances and provide one more way to draw closer to Him.

We should be aware of our tremendous blessings that enable us to read the Bible and worship in a country with the kind of freedom we have. When I think of how many Bibles are in each of our homes and the many countries around the world where the Bible is not available, I'm ashamed that I took God's Word for granted for so long.

4. I need to use what God has taught me by teaching others. Paul told Timothy to teach others what he had been taught, and be prepared to use God's Word with other people:

And the things you have heard me say in the presence of many witnesses entrust to reliable men who will also be qualified to teach others. 2 Timothy 2:2

Chapter Seven

Preach the Word; be prepared in season and out of season; correct, rebuke, and encourage—with great patience and careful instruction. 2 Timothy 4:2

Not everyone is a gifted teacher. Teaching is not my greatest gift either, yet I've discovered a truth about those who want to express God's word to others: Nobody learns more than the teacher. If you have the ability to study and understand Scripture, God may want you to be a teacher.

Whether it's working with a youth group, sharing life's lessons with business people, or reading Scripture to just one other person, God can use many of us to be a light to others.

A few years ago I was not able, nor was I willing, to teach. Now that I have come to grips with the need to spend time in God's Word and do some comprehensive study, God has given me a real confidence and desire to share His Word. However, teaching does carry some added responsibilities that the Bible clearly spells out. Those that teach have the serious duty to never distort or blaspheme the Scripture and to always hold it in high esteem.

Keep in mind that the blessings and opportunities provided through sharing what God has taught us can only increase our love for Him. These four keys regarding the reading of God's word have helped me become closer to my Lord.

FELLOWSHIP

My third outfielder, the right fielder, is called *fellowship*, or sometimes referred to as a covenant relationship. Right field is usually where the weak link on the team goes. The right fielder doesn't get much serious participation; however, without him, the team would be considerably weakened.

Fellowship likewise is a fragile link in the lives of most believers. Usually we look at fellowship as socializing or friendships—rarely does any depth of relationship exist. I'm not knocking social activities or the need to have friends in and out of the church. I understand the necessity of these kinds of relationships to broaden our horizons.

Yet many Christians fail to initiate meaningful relationships that demand commitment—the kind of covenant relationship Jonathan and David had in the old Testament. Take a few minutes to read 1 Samuel chapters 18-20. Think about the sacrifice Jonathan made for his friend David. Jonathan would be the natural successor to King Saul, yet he put aside any ambitions for the throne to help save his friend's life. Their relationship stretched beyond mere friendship into what can only be described as a covenant relationship.

A covenant relationship for a Christian normally starts within a group of people with whom you worship and who have a common belief in Jesus Christ. The importance of fellowship is revealed in the early church described in Acts 2. Those early believers were continually together praying, studying God's Word, drawing closer to God and to each other.

Throughout his writings the Apostle Paul urges believers to have fellowship. The author of Hebrews 10:23-25 proclaims:

Let us hold unswervingly to the hope we profess, for he who promised is faithful. And let us consider how we may spur one another on toward love and good deeds. Let us not give up meeting together, as some are in the habit of doing, but let us encourage one another—and all the more as you see the Day approaching.

God did not intend for us to live the Christian life alone. He gave us spouses, and next to our relationship with Him, this is our most precious gift. Do you have a loving, covenant relationship with your spouse? If you do, that's wonderful! If you don't, I suggest you pray to God for guidance. You can also find Christian books that offer insights on marriage enrichment.

I also believe the Lord wants us to have relationships with one or two individuals of the same gender who might be able to identify with our struggles and problems from the same perspective. Someone who can provide inspiration, a listening ear, encouragement, advise and accountability. Someone who can question our actions and maybe give us some direction, whether or not we ask for it.

> God did not intend for us to live the Christian life alone.

Chapter Seven

I see so many lonely people in the marketplace, it's absolutely tragic. Many of them are getting creamed every day and have nobody who will listen to them. They struggle with families, careers, and difficult decisions on the job, as well as their walk with the Lord.

I've had people invite me to breakfast or lunch only to discover that what they really wanted was someone to talk with, someone to listen to their troubles. They need a friend first of all, but they also need something beyond friendship. They need the kind of friend that can only come from a covenant relationship. The basics of this important alliance guarantees three things:

1. You'll always have a friend. Loneliness will continually be replaced with companionship. Although we're never really alone because we have God, it's still important to have close personal relationships.

 What a tremendous, comforting feeling to know that in sharing joy or sorrow, you're never alone. I'm not a psychologist, but I have to believe there would be a whole lot less depression in this world if people had the kind of friendship I'm talking about.

2. You'll always have encouragement. This is the sort of encouragement that comes as you inspire each other, pick each other up when you're down, and face trials and triumphs together. This motivates us to grow and reach new goals.

3. You'll always have someone to hold you accountable for your actions. This is one of the most important facets of a covenant relationship. Our friends hold us accountable for what we do, thereby helping us to remain focused and able to face the tough issues in life. Without this accountability, I believe it is impossible to maximize our potential.

Once one of my closest friends called and left a message of congratulations on my answering machine regarding a career move of mine. This was no ordinary message. In fact, he actually sang a song to me, long distance, wished me good luck, and reminded me, no matter how swept up I might get in this new move, never to forget my priorities. That's a real covenant friend.

Such friends ask each other hard questions, challenge decisions, and grow together. A relationship of this type does not happen overnight—it takes time and commitment. That's why so few really substantial friendships exist today. Most of us are not willing to commit ourselves to this extent.

Looking back at my own life, I realize I didn't even know what I was missing until I began to search in earnest for God's plan for my life. As those relationships developed in my life, I began to be much more open to what God might have me do. Today those relationships are vital to my well-being. Now as I look at my priorities of faith, family, friends, and vocation, I know how badly I need my wife and a group of friends in Christ to surround me, encourage me, give me leadership, and hold me accountable.

The New Testament makes it clear that God did not send men out alone. When Jesus started His ministry, He immediately surrounded Himself with the Apostles and sent them out to do God's work in teams.

On subsequent journeys Paul and Barnabas took companions. Throughout the New Testament the idea of men and women banding together for mutual encouragement and accountability is dominant. And when two or more are gathered in His name, there is a synergy that makes it easier to share the load. God's goals can be accomplished quicker by teamwork than by one person working alone.

I believe if we are to accomplish what God wants each of us to do, we must have the kind of encouragement and accountability that comes from relationships where people love and trust each other.

Chapter Seven

Before moving on, let's take one more look at our outfield:

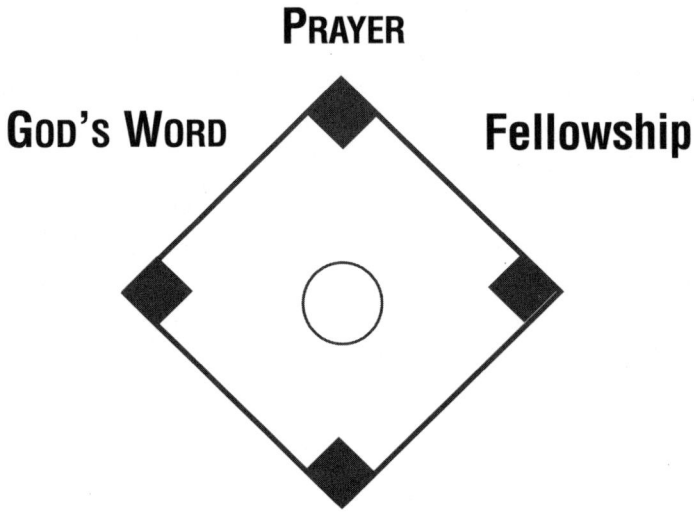

PRAYER

GOD'S WORD   **Fellowship**

Prayer plays the pivotal position (center field), but we need God's Word for specific direction (left field), and we need other believers for fellowship to encourage us and hold us accountable (right field). We must have all three to be really effective.

I believe as each of these three areas develop in our own lives, God will change our hearts, our directions, and our whole purpose of being. He will give us more of a desire to be conformed to the image of Jesus Christ. Only then will we have an opportunity to find His sovereign plan for our lives.

REFLECTIONS FOR THOUGHT

1. What does my prayer life look like today? Am I satisfied? Is God satisfied? How can I start improving my prayer life? Am I committed to building an intimate relationship with Jesus Christ?

2. Am I gaining ground in understanding God's plan for me through the Word? How can I start the process of studying the Bible? Am I beginning to see how the Bible can be my own personal spiritual plan?

3. Do I have a covenant relationship? A close friend? How can I begin to improve or find that relationship?

4. Am I willing to start improving all three? When?

SCRIPTURE REFERENCES

Philippians 4:6-7
Nehemiah
2 Timothy 3:16-17
2 Timothy 2:2
2 Timothy 4:2
1 Samuel chapters 18-20
Acts chapter 2
Hebrews 10:23-25

Chapter Eight

TIME FOR UPDATING OUR RESUME

*H*e was thirty-two years old. His conservative navy blue suit, white shirt, and striped tie were perfect for an interview. His résumé highlighting career accomplishments completed his professional presentation. He smiled. I wanted to say, "Lights . . . camera . . . action!"

Then I asked my favorite first question:"Tell me what you would like to accomplish in your life."

His smile gave way to a perplexed look, the shoulders sagged, and after what seemed like an eternity, in an almost inaudible voice he said, "I don't know."

I spent the next fifteen minutes helping this fellow regain his confidence. After we got over that hurdle, we were able to spend some quality time talking about what he needed to do to gain some insight into his future.

I would estimate 80 percent of the people I interview for our company are there because they are looking for a job, having given little thought to their careers, let alone any consideration as to what God's plans may be for their lives.

How will we understand our real mission?

111

Chapter Eight

All people, especially Christians, should have a plan for their lives. Our goals are important. We need to plan now for the future.

There are significant businesses in the marketplace today that produce good earnings ratios, maintain good employee relations, and give their stockholders a reasonable return on their investments. These companies have one thing in common—they know where they are going. They have a vision. They understand their purpose and, just as importantly, they have a strategic plan designed to help them accomplish their objectives.

Of course the strategic planning process has been around for years. It allows a company to analyze its strengths and weaknesses, take a good statistical and analytical view of the market, and then begin to establish a strategy to accomplish its vision. Through a strategic planning process, a business can determine a set of objectives that are well thought out and begin to set its direction.

Planning your life around a mission statement can be invaluable as you evaluate the abilities God has given you.

With this type of goal setting, companies can be more productive, more focused, and more likely to reach their goals. Otherwise an enterprise can easily lose its focus, become fractured, suffer poor productivity, and fail to achieve its potential. Without proper training and adequate tools for measurement, evaluation cannot exist. With an orderly strategy comes the potential for achieving, and even exceeding, goals.

Since most business leaders agree that it takes a mission statement to steer the course of a business, I have to ask why we don't offer a mission statement for our own personal lives. This could, indeed, make a difference in what we personally accomplish. To me it is a tragic that we don't know how to use those same concepts in our own personal lives. I struggle with this, too, yet I think the experiences God gives us in the marketplace should be used in every aspect of our daily living. Certainly these goals should embrace processes that encourage traits such as quality, value, and integrity.

Planning your life around a mission statement is a concept that can be invaluable as we review our own potential and evaluate the abilities and experiences God has given us. Through this process I believe our goals and priorities—personally, spiritually, and financially—will become evident.

Over the last several years two exercises—"The Evaluation Process" and "Developing Criteria for Career Selection"—have proven beneficial in helping me establish my own goals and priorities for living. By using these two processes, you should be able to articulate your mission in life because you'll know more about yourself.

THE EVALUATION PROCESS

Sit down with a pencil and two pieces of paper. List all your strengths on one sheet and all your weaknesses on the other. Keep each one limited to short phrases or sentences—not paragraphs—and keep it simple!

Remember God has given all of us certain abilities and, on the other hand, maybe a few "thorns" requiring diligence and patience for life. So, don't dwell on your strengths egotistically or your weaknesses negatively. Just list specific pluses and minuses.

Over the next few days and weeks, evaluate each strength and each weakness you identified. Pray about them. You will begin to see aspects of yourself that you had forgotten about or did not realize existed. Little pieces of your personality, dormant for years, might become more visible. You may see strengths more as assets that can be exploited. Weaknesses that have been obstacles may seem less formidable.

You will begin to think of ways to overcome, or at least compensate for, deficiencies that would have stopped you in the past. For example, instead of berating yourself by saying I *should* have been able to the job better, it's more helpful to ask yourself how you *could* have done it more efficiently. Through the process you will learn a lot about yourself and how God might be able to use you in significant ways, both in the marketplace and in ministry.

As your thoughts begin to crystallize and become clear, share them with your spouse or a good friend. Ask for feedback. You may find they have some interesting insights you have missed. If you agree, put their comments on your list.

Don't worry if your strength and weakness sheets keeps changing—they should! I'm convinced that if this process is done with a deep desire to know yourself better, you'll begin to get a more focused picture of who you really are.

DEVELOPING CRITERIA FOR CAREER SELECTION

Next you'll want to put together several criteria for career selection. This includes a list of what is in your heart regarding your career. Again, the process takes some time and cannot be done in one sitting. Indeed, it may not be completed in your life-time. This process needs to be thoughtfully prayed over for days, weeks, maybe months or years. It will require modifying and updating as you mature spiritually and professionally. Yet I believe if we have a heart to be where God wants us, we must take the time to ask ourselves some tough emotional and spiri-tual questions about our lives in the marketplace.

The developing of your "Criteria for Career Selection" process should entail a simple outline, a basic guideline of perhaps two sheets, with bullets beside each statement. It could have five parts or more. In the following example I've used what I call the "basic five" criteria:

1. What are your spiritual goals? Where does God want you to be? Will this job allow you to be the person He has called you to be in all areas of your life? Isn't it incredibly important that we ask that question and are honest with the answers before we accept a new job? Isn't it necessary that we ask that question in reviewing where we are today?

2. How can your gifts be utilized? God has given all of us beautiful gifts, and each one of us is different. I believe He wants us all to exploit those gifts for the Kingdom and in our vocation. Yes, He wants us to accomplish good things with our gifts. Simply put, does a new job or our current job allow us to do that? Your strength and weakness lists will give you great insight here.

3. What kind of business is appropriate for you? What kind of job possibility turns you on? For example, I am a marketing and idea man. I probably would be a poor accountant or engineer. Think about what you like and what you don't like, in terms of job descriptions. Remember you can also transfer skills from one job to another. A manager with organizational skills could also work in his or her own business, as the owner of a retail store. Professional career management counselors can help you address many of the issues faced during job transition.

4. What security aspects do you need? We do have the responsibility to ourselves and our families for stability and wholeness. Our goals must be balanced with career objectives that support both personal and family needs.

5. Does your job offer you personal satisfaction? Your work should be enjoyable and fulfilling. If your job brings you no personal satisfaction, then you are robbing yourself of your own spiritual potential. Friendships, career fulfillment, and satisfaction should be a part of the job.

My own growth process began with a lot of thought, prayer, and help from my wife and friends. As I personally began to look at my future after my employment at John Wanamaker's, my own "Criteria for Career Selection" evolved and became a mirror of my heart. I was blown away by the perceptions I learned about myself and what I really wanted in a career.

Below is the outline of my criteria for career selection:

I.   SPIRITUAL GOALS

Job must clearly be revealed to be a part of God's sovereign plan for my life.

A. Must allow me to continue to grow in my faith, to be more Christ-like each day.

B. Must allow me to continue to be a Christ-centered husband and father.

C. Must allow me to be God's servant in the marketplace.

D. Must allow me to serve in those ministries to which He has called me.

II. UTILIZATION OF GIFTS

Job must allow me to maximize the talents God gave me.

A. Leadership skills—job should put me in a position where I can be a point person for both the business and Kingdom work.

B. Strategic-planning skills—business should be one both needing and desiring short-term and long-term planning.

C. Communication skills—business should be one both needing and desiring an outstanding communicator for both associates and customers, an ambassador for the business.

D. Motivation skills—business should be one desiring motivation and execution of purpose.

III. PROFILE OF BUSINESS

Business must fit with my personal aspirations.

A. Must be a business with a significant future.

B. Must be a business where innovation and change are desired and accepted.

C. Must be a business where accomplishments are expected.

D. Must be a business with a sense of purpose.

IV. SECURITY INSIGHTS

Job must provide the opportunity for security, both financially and emotionally, for me and my family.

A. Compensation must be equitable for industry and position.

B. Compensation should be structured where business success is basis for equity or bonus.

C. My wife and children need to sense husband/father providing for their well-being, both financially and emotionally.

D. Career should give me a sense of security, a sense of inner peace and comfort.

V. CAREER FULFILLMENT

Job must offer personal satisfaction.

A. Work should be enjoyable and fulfilling.

B. Friendships would be developed.

C. Accomplishments would be recognized.

D. Job should bring a personal sense of satisfaction.

A real key in the development of your own career criteria will be your honesty and frankness. You may or may not like what you see, but that is the only way to begin to deal with the hard task of searching for God's priorities.

Having completed your strengths and weaknesses exercise, and using the "Criteria for Career Selection" as a guide, begin to think what your personal criteria will look like. It's exciting to know God will give you some amazing insights.

Don't feel locked into my format: you may have a different formula and certainly you'll have different priorities. What is important is that you begin to go through the process of exploring the question, "Where does God want me to be?"

Some excellent human resource tools are available to help through this process. Placement firms will often recommend a whole battery of tests to help your process of career evaluation. However, never forget the importance of your own career criteria, as well as those thoughts God shares with you through prayer. These keep the process from being mechanical. We do not have a mechanical God, and He desires to be a part of this process. After all, it is His plan for our lives!

Write your own criteria for career selection below. Remember: Each person's priorities are different. Some may value security over all else, while others want the freedom to use their entrepreneurial gifts. There is no right or wrong decision here, so feel free to choose what suits you best.

> Begin to go through the process of exploring the question, "Where does God want me to be?"

PERSONAL CRITERIA FOR CAREER SELECTION FOR (YOUR NAME)

I. **SPIRITUAL GOALS**

    A.

    B.

    C.

    D.

II. **UTILIZATION OF GIFTS**

    A.

    B.

    C.

    D.

III. **PROFILE OF BUSINESS**

    A.

    B.

    C.

    D.

IV. **SECURITY INSIGHTS**

    A.

    B.

    C.

    D.

V. **CAREER FULFILLMENT**

    A.

    B.

    C.

    D.

The "Criteria for Career Selection" process helped me do four things in my job search after the selling of John Wanamaker's:

1. Focus on the exact types of companies and positions I sought.

2. Become more productive in seeking the right position.

3. Feel new confidence because of the process I had gone through to find my way.

4. Attain an attitude of prayer.

God had the opportunity to enlighten me as I thought through my life with Him. He gave me a new love for the words found in Jeremiah 29:11-13 (Living Bible):

For I know the plans I have for you, says the Lord. They are plans for good and not for evil, to give you a future and a hope. In those days when you pray, I will listen. You will find me when you seek me, if you look for me in earnest.

GOING ALL OUT FOR A NEW CAREER

As I prepared to leave John Wanamaker's, I had already begun the interviewing process with several companies. Although some attractive positions were opening, I knew the fit was not right. I could not put my finger on any one reason because on the surface everything looked great—attractive compensation, nice perks, and status.

However, as I completed the process of determining my career criteria, it all started to click and make sense. As I laid out my strengths and weaknesses and compared my experience with the jobs and companies I was pursuing, I found all sorts of mismatches. My career criteria sheet pointed out why these opportunities were wrong for me.

Recently I was telling a friend how difficult it is to put into writing what's in your heart, especially when it comes to dreams and goals for the future. Many times the world will try to crowd out what you know is right and tempt you with money, fame, or security.

Chapter Eight

Nothing is wrong with any of those unless you forsake what is right for you to achieve them. This is especially true for Christians. I believe we have that responsibility to Christ in the marketplace. It is virtually impossible to fulfill that responsibility without knowing if we are in the right place.

In my life, I've seen a lot of people, some of them Christians, with their backs to the wall, having to make decisions about their futures and careers, so I know how important a process like determining career criteria can be.

Few people take the time or are given the opportunity to evaluate themselves and possible employers, let alone ponder where God would want them to be.

Today, families move, friendships are disrupted, and risks are commonplace. All too often this results in disenchantment, unfulfilled dreams, and frustration.

 A couple of years ago a non-Christian friend called and was explaining his thoughts about changing jobs. The new position was a nice jump in his career path, the pay was attractive, the location was pretty good, and the company was secure. As we talked about the move, it was clear he had not considered if this was the kind of job he wanted for the long term. Not having a faith, he was not concerned about where God wanted him to be, either.

"Isn't this just more of the same stuff you've been doing the last few years?" I asked him. "You've complained about retail being so cyclical, about working for a large corporation, and about how boxed in you've felt. Now you've been offered a bigger title and more pay, but basically it's the same deal."

After a long pause he answered, "I wish I hadn't called you." He took the job anyway. Eighteen months later he left that job to chase another dream.

Too often I find Christians who think the same way as my friend. We need to be challenged to be where God wants us. He doesn't want us to chase dreams that aren't His.

In today's volatile market, where company downsizing is the norm, none of us knows when we might face the dilemma of losing our jobs. This may mean switching jobs, perhaps several times over the years. If that happens, mapping out your "Criteria for Career Selection" ahead of time will help you during these important junctures.

If we truly believe Jeremiah 29:11-13, that God has a sovereign plan for our lives, then surely some process is necessary to validate that we are where God wants us to be. I would like to encourage you to take some time and start that process now.

God doesn't want us to chase dreams that aren't His.

Chapter Eight

REFLECTIONS FOR THOUGHT

1. Write down your strengths and weaknesses. Share your strengths and weaknesses with your spouse or a Christian friend. Ask for feedback. Reflect on their thoughts.

2. Put together your own criteria for career selection. Through these processes, you may find you are right where God wants you, or you may find He has other plans for you.

3. Pray for God's guidance. Ask yourself, "Is this God's plan for my life?

4. After completing these steps, see if you can write your own personal mission statement.

SCRIPTURE REFERENCES

Jeremiah 29:11-13

Chapter Nine

THE BEATITUDES AND THE MARKETPLACE

How should The Beatitudes affect the way we look at today's free enterprise system?

I believe God chose me to be part of the free enterprise system for a reason—just as He may have chosen you. When we begin to understand that we are really missionaries in the marketplace, everything we do takes on a whole new meaning.

I know I don't have all the answers; I have to admit I'm just beginning to learn more about Him. Yet, each day, I feel that I'm getting more in touch with what I think He wants from me. This is all God asks from us: that we become aware of Him and our place in His plan.

As God set my heart on trying to articulate my road map for life in the marketplace, it became easier for me to find encouragement, strength, and wisdom to make the right decisions. Time after time I was brought back to a piece of Scripture I love so much: "The Beatitudes" that are included in the Sermon on the Mount. I've often thought about how Jesus would have applied that famous and powerful sermon to today's business world. Think about your own experiences, and then look at the great message Christ gave us and see how it might work for you.

123

Chapter Nine

THE FIRST BEATITUDE

Blessed are the poor in spirit, for theirs is the kingdom of heaven. Matthew 5:3

The marketplace, being secular, simply does not have a spiritual dimension to it. However, in all of The Beatitudes Jesus was giving us a new order. We deal with ego, pride, greed, and power every day in the business world. Some people follow the dog-eat-dog philosophy that says "Get all you can today, even if it means doing in the other guy."

> I believe God chose me to be part of the free enterprise system for a reason, just as He may have chosen you.

Everything the marketplace covets has to do with success and affluence. Indeed, material accomplishments are sometimes our only measuring stick. Yet Jesus was saying, "You have nothing if you have success and don't have Me, but you have everything if you have Me, regardless of whether you have success." In our constant pursuit of excellence, we sometimes lose our desire to be His person. In so doing, we lose our center. There are times I think He wants us to admit our humility, our failures, and our disappointments.

These "down" times allow us to see more clearly those things that have real meaning for us. Jesus, himself, never had an easy path to follow. I am sure he had his disappointments, too. He knew that what he was doing ran contrary to the opinions of public officials. Yet, despite the dangers, he continued to do His work. He didn't fail in his mission. Like Jesus, when you take a stand for what is right, it may appear that you have failed in the eyes of the world, but in God's eyes you have succeeded.

Father, I pray that I might die to myself and I might focus my eyes on you. I would pray that I would be a person that understands that every talent and piece of wealth that I have was given to me by you. Let me be a person who radiates a humbleness, a humility in spirit, a desire to be your servant. And Lord, might I give all my success back to you. Amen.

THE SECOND BEATITUDE

Blessed are those who mourn, for they will be comforted.
Matthew 5:4

I can't count the number of times I've thanked God for this great little piece of Scripture and the many others found throughout the Bible that are so comforting in difficult times. Many of the major characters of the Bible had some significant down times in their lives. The common thread that binds all these men and women together is how they were drawn to God in great crisis.

So it is for those of us that are called to work in the marketplace. We must endure the roller-coaster ride that our free enterprise system gives us—complete with potholes big enough to swallow us whole. Whether we must deal with job loss, labor strikes, boredom, or difficult people, we need to realize that we are working through God's holy and sovereign plan for us. He has a purpose and He has called us to be a part of it.

When we're down and our backs are against the wall, God has promised that if we focus on Him, He will draw us to Himself and He will grow our character. He has also promised to give us a great comfort that we could not get elsewhere. I could not have survived without a relationship with Jesus Christ. When I needed Him, I felt Him standing next to me. This is something I love to share with people wherever I go.

Father, let me be thankful for the down times, the valleys, the deserts of my life. Let me praise you for your comfort, your compassion, your strength. But most of all, thank you Father for molding me to be the person you desire. Amen.

THE THIRD BEATITUDE

Blessed are the meek, for they will inherit the earth. Matthew 5:5

For many years I had trouble understanding this Beatitude. Then one Sunday morning, our pastor was in the fourth chapter of Ephesians and he gave us the Greek definition of "meek." It was "strength under control."

Chapter Nine

All of a sudden I realized that God was talking about a disciplined person—one who can control his or her emotions and who, by virtue of character, is taller than the world's temptations.   The world says be noisy and brash, bend the rules, break the vows, accomplish at all costs, be hard and tough and mighty and powerful. Yet God has called upon us to think eternally—not transiently. To put character and integrity before goals. To be kind and sensitive, and humble and teachable, so that we can truly gain His kingdom on earth.

I think of what would happen to our country's major corporations if they were run on the basis of the third Beatitude. It might be possible that people would be more excited about working for other people, and that billions of dollars would be spent honestly rather than fraudulently.

If we understood what God really meant by "meek," we would know that what He wants is powerful men and women ready to stand in the gap for Him—people who attain their power not from material success but from the Holy Spirit that dwells within.

Father, now I come to you and would pray that you would make me a disciplined person; a person strong enough to resist temptation; a person that acknowledges a need for you; and a person that is kind and sensitive and understands that people are more important than things. I would pray that you would make me a meek warrior for your kingdom. Amen.

THE FOURTH BEATITUDE

Blessed are those who hunger and thirst for righteousness, for they will be filled. Matthew 5:6

I sometimes think our free enterprise system is like one big football field, with business men and women making all the running plays. Yet, I have to wonder what we're all running for. Perhaps we're running for wealth or fame—two really big ego-satisfiers. We may be running for power and the control that goes with it. Then there's security, without which many people believe they would be lost. Lastly, there are those who drive themselves hard for success and achievement at any cost.

In this Beatitude, Jesus is saying that if you seek His standards, His will, and His sovereign plan, you will find great peace. As a contrast, it seems to me that peace eludes us, for the faster we run, the less satisfied we are.

I've seen people attain great wealth, fame, and power, but many of them are unhappy and unable to find peace within themselves because their priorities are set solely on secular rather than spiritual goals. Yet money itself is not inherently bad if it is put to good use, especially if it is achieved with a reliance on God and the idea that it can be applied to helping others.

If you're lucky enough to wake up to the fact that you may be throwing away your life on irrelevant pursuits, then don't look back! Just praise God for sounding the alarm.

If we focus our lives on Christ, we will have a tremendous peace and satisfaction, regardless of whether we achieve the world's aspirations or not. Just that promise in this Beatitude should give us a great confidence in the days ahead.

Father, we come to you seeking the strength that we will need to be righteous people.

We come to you and ask for your forgiveness, as the world has crowded you out of our lives with its goals and priorities. Give us a vision of what it will be like to be righteous people. Give us that sense of peace and satisfaction that you've promised. Let us feel your love and compassion as we strive to be the people you've called us to be. Amen.

THE FIFTH BEATITUDE

Blessed are the merciful, for they will be shown mercy.
Matthew 5:7

I remember what one of my Bible study leaders, a wise man in his seventies, told me about the fifth Beatitude. He said, "Jeff, we so easily forget when our Savior was hung on the cross, brutally whipped, mocked with a crown of thorns, betrayed by a close friend, and deserted by His disciples. He looked down at all of those who were watching him die and said, 'Father, forgive them, for they know not what they do' [Luke 23:34]. Our Jesus is the master of forgiveness. Our Jesus is the master of mercy. We could never begin to be merciful enough to gain the mercies that He has given us."

Yet Jesus has called us also to be merciful, to be people who really care. In the marketplace this means encouraging those who are struggling, and accepting and loving those who aren't very lovable.

According to this Beatitude, we need to show compassion and manage people with a fairness and sensitivity that reflects the teachings of Jesus. And we should do this not because we expect something from Him, but because that's His law and that's the way He wants us to be.

When I think of the thousands of people who have been destroyed emotionally and physically by the lack of sensitivity from business people, I see what Jesus was saying.

We need to show compassion and manage people with a fairness and sensitivity that reflects the teachings of Jesus.

It's not hard to figure out why people are not loyal to companies or to the system responsible for such callousness.

What would it be like, I wonder, if we lived in a country where a free enterprise system meant that we could be merciful to others? Think of the tremendous loyalties that would be built among associates! In all probability management and labor would no longer need two separate organizations to negotiate a contract. They could establish a set of principles based on mutual trust and understanding. Think of the tremendous energy that could be utilized if people knew and understood the mercies Jesus is talking about in this Beatitude.

Jesus promised us that mercy will be rewarded with mercy. A person who conducts his or her business affairs with forbearance toward associates and customers will be rewarded. Those rewards may not always be monetary, nor will you always be able to put them back on the balance sheet, but your heart and spirit will be rewarded. You will know without any doubt that God has rejoiced in your actions.

Father, we thank you for this great Beatitude and we can never praise you enough for the mercies you have extended to us: the mercy of salvation and eternal life. We would pray in our understanding of this Beatitude that our lives might be embraced by a desire to be merciful, sensitive, and kind to all of those you have placed around us—in our families, our business-es, and our professions. Amen.

THE SIXTH BEATITUDE

Blessed are the pure in heart, for they will see God. Matthew 5:8

One of the things I hear Christian business people say most often is, "I don't really sense God in my life." I think the key question here is, do we really want to see God? I know there have been times in my life when I've talked about having a desire to see God, but in reality there was so much of *the world* in my life that I *couldn't* see Him. I knew that, in order to see God, I was going to have to eliminate many things I thought were important. We must first have a real desire to want God in our lives, above all else, in order to take action.

Four points have significantly helped me to think through this process. The first is dealing with sin. Perhaps the reason we haven't dealt with sin is because we actually may like it. It may mean a significant change in our lifestyle, and a change in our friends. But I think Jesus is saying that in order to see Him, we need to put virtue above vice.

The second is *defining our goals.* There may be many goals that are not Christ-centered in our lives. My own goals were self-centered, ego-centered, and it wasn't until I saw them in relation to eternal life that I began to see the vision God might have for me.

The third point is that we need to *surround ourselves with Christian fellowship.* This kind of quality friendship enables us to gain clarity in a marketplace filled with temptations that can consume us. If we are surrounded by others who do not have moral motives, we run the risk of assuming their goals for our-selves. Without a quality Christian fellowship, we don't have a chance of succeeding. If we can have that kind of friendship in the workplace, terrific! If not, we have to go elsewhere to find it.

Lastly, if we aspire to seek God, we need to *take a step of faith with Him.* We need to be bold enough to step out, knowing our success or failure is in His hands. By the world's standards, what we're doing may not make sense, but in our hearts we know it's what God wants us to do. We need to move ahead, knowing the only way we can succeed will be through God's sovereignty. Once we set out on the path, there's no going back.

Father, we would now come to you and ask you to cleanse the motives of our hearts. We would ask you to give us a great conviction to see you and be your servant. We would come to you and ask you to give us the courage, the stamina, and the wisdom to be the men and women you desire us to be. We would pray that we might see you as we begin that process in a new and significant way. Then we would have the desire to share your faithfulness with the world wherever we go. Amen.

THE SEVENTH BEATITUDE

Blessed are the peacemakers, for they will be called sons of God. Matthew 5:9

Today's newspapers are filled with conflict. Hatred, misunderstanding, and physical and emotional abuse create front-page news. In this Beatitude, Jesus makes it clear that we don't need to be part of the dissension. That we can stand in the gap for Him.

Yet Christians are often part of the problem, sometimes instigating friction by their very actions. Our free enterprise system, riddled with backbiting and infighting, has become weakened to the point where Pacific Rim and European manufacturing companies have made strong inroads into our economy.

The continual distrust between labor and management, along with lack of company productivity and loss of security for company employees, has caused people to lose their enthusiasm for the marketplace.

Yet frequently when there has been an opportunity for Christians to be the reconcilers and to stand up for what is right, we seem to have forgotten the purpose that God has given us.

Think of your own company and your job in that company. Then think about the opportunities and the privileges God may have given you to be a peacemaker in the past few months. How exciting it would be to have the opportunity to be reunite those who have been disconnected through misunderstanding and to know that with the help of Jesus Christ, you will be able to accomplish the task that He has given you.

Father, I would come to you now and I would pray with a fervent heart that the hostility and the anger that is in my own heart be dissolved, and in its place you would give me a heart to be a reconciler, to be a healer, to be a person that is absolutely committed to your will. Let me take each situation of conflict that you place in my life and let me treat it as if it is sacred. Let me be the person you call to stand in the gap, to bring people together, to serve as your peacemaker. Amen.

THE EIGHTH BEATITUDE

Blessed are those who are persecuted because of righteousness, for theirs is the kingdom of heaven. Matthew 5:10

Most of us have spent our lives protecting ourselves. We've worried a great deal about where we're going to live, how to keep the roof over our heads, and how to save our jobs so we can retire with a nice pension plan.

This isn't necessarily wrong unless taken to extremes. However, we do put forth a lot of time and energy providing ourselves with material security instead of concerning ourselves more with our spiritual strength.

In the early days, Christians were persecuted for their beliefs. Fortunately today we live in a society where we may practice the faith of our choice. And we've gotten so used to religious freedom in this country that we tend to be complacent.

Persecution today comes in a more subtle guise. Today we aren't hung on a cross or stoned to death if we speak out. Today we can be fired, ignored, not promoted, and ostracized by so-called friends.

When we stand up for our beliefs, it is still risky business, but only in terms of material success. Today our values no longer reflect whether we live or die as a result of our faith; it has all come down to the issue of whether we do something for love or for money. You can tweak your value system and not break any laws except the moral ones God has set down for you. You can look the other way when a wrong is being done, but you still have to face yourself in the mirror each day.

Think for a minute about your career and some of the experiences you've had recently. Have you had the honor to suffer for Christ? Did you take the world's road to avoid persecution? We all take business risks each day, but how much are you willing to risk for Christ? Jesus asked Peter to walk on water, and yet most of us have trouble when He just takes our oars away.

Jesus said to us in this Beatitude, "Step out of the boat. Be bold for me. Be willing to be persecuted. Be prepared to suffer and you will see the Kingdom of Heaven." Some might call that radical theology. But whatever we want to call it, let's not be confused: It is our Father's Word.

Father, I pray that you might prepare me to be a person to stand in the gap for you. Give me a deep desire to be obedient to your will, regardless of the circumstances. Father, prepare me to serve you even if that might mean persecution or suffering. But let me feel your deep love, your protection, your compassion, and let me fully understand your promise to be faithful. Amen.

The Sermon on the Mount is a new law for today just as Jesus gave it to His disciples 2000 years earlier. Is it applicable for us? You bet it is! Let's meditate on it and know that we are ready to be part of this exciting and timeless direction from our Master.

REFLECTIONS FOR THOUGHT

1. Which Beatitude challenges me the most? Why? What am I going to do about it?

2. How are the Beatitudes relevant to me today?

3. Would reflecting on the eight prayers for the next month help?

4. How can I share these Beatitudes with a Christian friend?

SCRIPTURE REFERENCES

Matthew 5:3-10

Chapter Ten

WHERE DO WE GO FROM HERE?

W riting this book has been a process that has encouraged me to be more like the man God desires. When I began my odyssey, I drew a little closer to Christ, but I know and He knows that I'm still a long way from home. What encourages me most is that, through His grace, I've been able to start the journey. As the father of two children, nothing thrills me more than to know my youngsters are headed in the right direction. I know our Father in heaven would say the same of us.

I believe the marketplace is exactly where God has called me to be and, in making the commitment to Him, I sense a real comfort and peace with my place in life.

If you feel that same sense of serenity, then I congratulate you on starting your journey. It's my hope that some of my own experiences might help you along the way.

If, however, you feel that life is going nowhere, and you're getting tired of the same old treadmill, my prayer for you is that this writing might encourage you to evaluate your need to make a new start.

Beginning the journey.

Chapter Ten

The first, and most important, question to ask yourself is this:

Do I know Christ as my Savior?

Although this book was written on the premise that its readers would be Christians, I understand that there will be those who have not made that decision. For me this was the starting point in life — that day when I said, "Jesus accept me for who I am, be the focus of my life, and give me the wisdom and courage to be the person you desire." This cornerstone decision, is the place to begin in your life, just as I did.

Next, ask yourself:

Is this where God wants me to be?

Some of the material in the preceding chapters may have given you insight for answering this question. If God has given you a peace about where you are today, your new goal may simply mean becoming a more active participant. If you question your place in life today, I encourage you to aggressively look for God's direction.

Finally, ask yourself:

Are you growing each day to be more like Him?

What a wonderful sense of inner joy we have when we know that our dreams are His desires!

This is where we gain our peace and fulfillment in life. What a wonderful sense of inner joy we have when we know that our dreams are His desires!

I believe God has a mission for each of us. He has extended the invitation; now it's up to us to accept.

Be assured that no matter where you are today, He loves you, and through His grace, anything is possible. It is His word (and my cornerstone scripture) that encourages us all:

For I know the plans I have for you, says the Lord. They are plans for good and not for evil, to give you a future and a hope. In those days when you pray, I will listen. You will find me when you seek me, if you look for me in earnest.
Jeremiah 29:11-13 *(Living Bible)*

I wish you well on your journey!

ABOUT
THE AUTHOR

Jeffrey Comment's understanding of the challenges facing today's workplace professional spans nearly thirty years of management experience. As chairman and CEO of Helzberg Diamonds, an eighty-year-old Kansas City-based subsidiary of Berkshire Hathaway, Inc., his uncompromising approach to business ethics have made him one of his community's most sought-after speakers and civic leaders.

Jeffrey W. Comment
Chairman &
CEO of
Helzberg
Diamonds

Jeff's organizational affiliations are far reaching. In addition to being a director of the Greater Kansas City Chamber of Commerce, the Civic Council of Greater Kansas City, and the Kansas City United Way, he also chairs boards for the Private Industry Council and the Kansas City Minority Supplier Development Council. In addition, he is the former chairman of the National Board of Young Life.

Married for twenty-five years to his wife Martha and the father of Kristen and Ryan, Jeff is a business leader who believes that one must be accountable for one's actions, both to family and associates. He takes his leadership role seriously and considers personal and company mission statements critical to the health of the American workplace.

137

About The Author

"Mission statements provide focus and a way to measure performance in business," he says. "As a Christian, I believe that we need to have a mission for our personal lives as well, so that we can maintain the integrity and moral stature that has characterized our country's history. To do this, we must live and do business as if the moral fabric of our lives depended on it—because it does."

For everyone who has wondered how America can hope to regain its image as the world's conscientious standard-bearer and how the nation can recapture its global leadership, Jeffrey Comment's Mission in the Marketplace is must reading.

ABOUT THE OTHERS WHO WORKED ON THIS BOOK

Jim Hughey is Vice President of University Advancement at LeTourneau University in Longview, Texas. He also served in the advancement area at Dallas Theological Seminary for eight years. Jim's experience in the marketplace includes sales and management work with a national manufacturer. He was a founder and partner in a regional manufacturing business in East Texas and has been involved in the creation and production of videos and study material to encourage and assist men and women serving Jesus Christ in the marketplace. Jim and his wife Mary live in Longview with their four children.

Shifra Stein is the author of many regional and national books as well as numerous articles that have appeared in magazines and newspapers across the country. The former Entertainment Editor and Restaurant Critic of The Kansas City Star newspapers, Shifra is a member of the Society of American Travel Writers and the Midwest Travel Writers Association and holds a fellowship from the University of Missouri-Kansas City's Greater Kansas City Writing Project. She conducts seminars and workshops on journaling for personal and spiritual growth in conjunction with churches, counseling organizations, career outplacement firms, and colleges.

About The Author

Mike Anderson is an independent creative director who has coordinated projects for dozens of Kansas City-area clients since the early 1980s. Prior to this he was the Creative Writing Manager for Hallmark Cards, Inc. Mike and his wife Pat have two grown sons, Colin and Nathan, and are active in Christian ministry through their church in Olathe, Kansas.

THE APPENDIX

OUR MISSION

To serve each and every customer in a very special way, always reflecting our 80 year heritage of excellence and value.

Sincerely,

Jeffrey W. Comment
Chairman and Chief Executive Officer

Framed and posted in every Helzberg Diamonds Jewelry Store for our Customers

See Chapter One, Page 9, Last Paragraph

AS A REMINDER OF OUR PROMISE TO OUR VALUED CUSTOMERS...

OUR MISSION

To serve each and every customer in a very special way, always reflecting our 80 year heritage of excellence and value.

HOW WE WILL ACCOMPLISH IT

A Human Resource strategy that proactively hires, trains, develops and challenges our people to be the most skilled associate team in every responsibility throughout the company.

A Merchandising strategy which provides the most dominant assortment of quality jewelry.

A Pricing strategy which offers the best value to our customers.

A Marketing strategy which is customer driven, creative and clearly communicates the strengths of our company.

A Real Estate strategy which creates an atmosphere of quality and service, positioned in markets for maximum productivity.

An Information Services strategy which enables our company to proactively manage our business.

OUR EXPECTATIONS...

The sales leader in every market we serve

A return on investment that exceeds industry standards and satisfies our investors' goals.

Jeffrey W. Comment
Chairman and Chief Executive Officer

Posted in the back office of each of our stores for our Associates

143

Inter-Office Memo

TO: All Stores   June 28, 199?

FROM: R. Associate

RE: XYZ Address

Why this memo? To expedite processing of information mailed to XYZ Corporation.

To provide Helzberg Diamonds with the best possible service, XYZ has requested we send correspondence, including any updated cutomer information to:

> XYZ Corporation
> P.O. Box 1114
> Anytown, MO 64000-1234

Thanks for your assistance and please feel free to call if you have any questions.

R. Associate, ext. 100

cc: General Office Management
    XYZ Corporation

HELZBERG DIAMONDS CODE OF ETHICS

Helzberg Diamonds enjoys a reputation for employing people of good character and morals, while ethically conducting its business for customers and associates.

In that spirit the Company has created the "Helzberg Diamonds Code of Ethics," which identifies each associate's moral responsibilities to the Company and its customers.

It is important each associate fully understands each code and what it stands for as we conduct our business. Each of these codes is covered in detail in the Helzberg Diamonds Policy Handbook or the Loss Prevention Manual. Questions regarding more specific detail should be directed to your immediate supervisor.

As a Helzberg Diamonds Associate, I will:

1. At all times conduct myself in an honest, professional manner, both with customers and fellow associates.

2. Always be mindful of our Company's fine reputation in all my actions, both in and out of the workplace.

3. Exercise my responsibility to protect the merchandise and property assets of the Company.

4. Comply with all Company policies and procedures.

5. Under no circumstances remove Company money, merchandise, or property from premises, falsify Company documents, or in any way willfully create erroneous Company information.

6. Communicate to management all situations where I perceive Company policy violations have taken place or where assets have potential for loss.

7. Under no circumstances represent the Company while under the influence of alcohol or illegal drugs/

Helzberg Diamonds will fully support our associate's efforts to comply with the Code of Ethics and will not tolerate any retribution for actions taken to meet these commitments.

This document is distributed to all associates annually. Please acknowledge your receipt of this document and understanding of these codes with your signature below. Return the signed document to the Human Resource Department.

Associate Name (Print)   Associate #   Date

Associate Signature   Store Name and Number

June Quiet Time

KC 5/30, 5/31 ~~commitment b/l~~

A. Request My Fathers Presence
B. Praise (Lord of Lords, King of Kings, God of Univ)
   1. Sovereign, Loving, Forgiving
   2. Salvation, Eternal Life
   3. Family (Martha, Kiki, Ryan)
   4. Friends (Russ, Neil, Tim)
   5. Health, Safety
   6. Material Blessings, Helzbergs ~~Jeremiah 29:11-13~~
   7. Plan For My Life -
   8. Yesterdays Gifts and Trials
C. Repentence
   1. Yesterdays Sin - Forgiveness.
   2. Todays Temptation - Protection
   3. Tomorrows Victory - Restoration
D. Personal Petitions
   1. Relationship with ~~You~~ Father
      a. ~~Prayer~~ (Each Day, Devotional
      b. ~~Scripture~~ (Psalms, Acts)
      c. ~~Fellowship~~ (Accountability
   2. Protection From Vices
      a. Materialism (House, Condo, A
      b. Anger (Emotions, Anger.)
         (Thoughts, Actions
                        A. contrl)

146